National Certificate of Educational Achievement · Lev

Achieving in English

L. Davis

Edited by David Wort M.A. Dip. Tch.

Achieving in English prepares candidates for NCEA Level 1 English

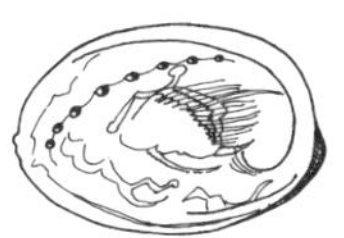

Printed and bound in Malaysia through Bookpac Production Services, Singapore.

Published by Sigma Publications Ltd
P.O. Box 15-248 Tauranga, New Zealand
Phone 0800 274 462   Fax 0800 274 460

ISBN 0-9582383-0-8

Contents

Contents

AS 1.6 - Unfamiliar Texts - continued

AS 1.7 - Deliver a Speech*

AS 1.8 - Media or Dramatic Presentation*

AS 1.9 - Research and Present Information*

* AS with green headings are internally assessed.

Text Suggestions

Here is a short list of texts suitable for study at Level 1 NCEA English. Other texts may be used.

Novels : *Tomorrow When the War Began*, *Letters from the Inside*, *See Ya Simon*

Non-Fiction : *I Know Why the Caged Bird Sings*, *Eruera*, *Krystyna's Story*

Plays : *Alive*, *Rosie*

Short Stories : *New Anthology of NZ Short Stories*, *Stories by Willie Davis, Owen Marshall Jane Westaway, Witi Ihimaera, Patricia Grace*

Films and TV : *Muriel's Wedding*, *What's Eating Gilbert Grape*, *Schindler's List*

Poetry : *NZ Poets - Apirana Taylor, Hone Tuwhare*

Newspapers & Magazines : *North & South, Mana, Metro*

4 Starting the Process

Even the best writers make a plan of what they want to write about. This helps to get their thoughts in order. Having decided on the viewpoint you wish to take, you need to note down broadly the elements of the story you will tell. This is the skeleton of the tale before you flesh it out with detail. Remember to relate to your own experiences as much as possible.

A A Skeleton Plan

The broad elements of the topic 'Break-up of a Friendship' could be the following:

Break-up of a Friendship

a) Initial situation. Setting. At a party.
b) The conflict arises. Quarrel. Who is involved?
c) Resolution of situation. How did it end?

1 Write briefly the broad elements you could follow when writing creatively about these topics.

Being a Victim

a) ....
b) ....
c) ....

A Courageous Rescue

a) ....
b) ....
c) ....

Given a Difficult Choice

a) ....
b) ....
c) ....

A Favourite View

a) ....
b) ....
c) ....

A Special Moment

a) ....
b) ....
c) ....

B Fleshing It Out

1 Choose one of the topics in A and put some flesh on the skeleton by following the guides given. Enter the chosen topic in this space:

a) WHAT happened?

....
....
....

b) WHEN did it happen?

....
....
....

c) WHY did it happen?

....
....
....

d) WHERE did it happen?

....
....
....

e) HOW did it happen?

....
....
....

f) WHAT was the result?

....
....
....

Intended Audience

Before beginning, you must decide for whom you are writing. Most essays at this level are for teenagers or adults and consequently a more sophisticated language and level of interest is required. The person reading the completed work will expect the vocabulary used to be compatible with their level of understanding and will consider this when judging the effectiveness of the writing as a whole.

A For Whom

The assessment instructions usually tell you for whom you are writing. eg "Your readers are other students and your teacher."

1 For each example of writing, place a 'C' for child, 'T' for teenager or 'A' for adult in the box.

a) "Hey, Hemi, wat'cha doing? Feel like a swim?" ☐

b) "I don't think that's appropriate. You need to revise your ideas." ☐

c) "Look at the kitten. Don't touch it. It might scratch." ☐

d) The little rabbit sat quietly nibbling on a carrot. Nibble, nibble, it went. ☐

e) He balanced lightly on the edge of the skatebowl, like a butterfly pausing on a leaf. ☐

f) It has to be appreciated that she spoke with great venom to those who stood by and did nothing. ☐

g) "It's cool. Don't worry about it. It's not the end of the world." ☐

h) Confidentially, there is a requirement that must be attended to immediately. ☐

i) A wee little house for a wee little mouse stood beside a wee little tree. ☐

B "Some Creep ..."

1 You have had a new pair of school shoes taken from your bag while at PE. Show the different levels of language you would use when explaining your loss to

a) A friend in your class.

....

....

b) Your PE teacher.

....

....

You should be able to see clearly from your answers the different levels of language used because the audience is different.

2 What differences can you see in your answers for a) and b) above? Look for differences such as cliches, tone, colloquialisms and sentence length, and explain how these affect the language levels.

a) ....

....

....

b) ....

....

....

C Understanding the Audience

1 Choose one of the following topics by circling it, then write a strong introductory sentence using the language level suitable for each age-group given.

Birthdays   School Days   Fright and Fear

Child ....

....

Teen ....

....

Adult [✓ Checkpoint in answers] ....

....

6 Purpose of Writing

Every writer has a purpose in writing. It may be to keep the reader interested and involved, to create mood and atmosphere, to evoke sympathy, to create humour or to cause a change in attitude of the reader.

A Using Mood

1 Label each of these extracts with one of the words in the box to show the mood the author has created in their writing.

Sympathetic Humorous Menacing

a) *'She became aware that someone was standing very close to her desk. She looked up. It was Mary glaring down at her.'*

The purpose of this extract is to create a .... mood.

b) *'Mihi started to sob harder, thinking of the times she had shared with her Mum - sometimes a tyrant, most times a compassionate parent with unpleasant vices.'*

This writing wants the reader to be ....

c) *'I'm not so good at homework, so it didn't surprise me when my teacher blew me up for not handing in my short story. What did surprise me though, was when she pulled out a huge knife, placed it on the desk and told me to finish the short story tonight or she'd cut off both my hands.'*

This extract is .... in intention.

d) Write two sentences that create a menacing mood.

....

....

....

....

....

B What to Choose?

1 Choose one of the following purposes in writing and show your understanding of what is required by writing an example of your own in that vein. Write the purpose you have chosen in a) and your example in b).

to influence	to entertain
to persuade	to create mood
to amuse	to create sympathy
to change an attitude	

a) The purpose I have chosen is ....

....

b) [✓ Checkpoint in answers] ....

....

....

....

....

....

....

....

....

....

....

....

....

....

C Finer Feelings

1 The choice of words may indicate feelings and attitudes. For each neutral word indicate one or two words that are either favourable or unfavourable choices that would influence the reader.

Favourable	→	Neutral	→	Unfavourable
a) large, chubby		a) overweight		a) fat, corpulent
b)		b) hungry		b) ....
c)		c) thin		c) ....
d)		d) kill		d) ....
e)		e) drunk		e) ....

Point of View

Before beginning writing you need to decide through what point of view the story is to be told. This is the narrative perspective of a story. It is important that once the point of view has been chosen, you keep to it.

A Many Angles

1 From whose point of view could a story about a rugby or netball game be written? List all those who could write about the game.

a) ....

b) ....

c) ....

d) ....

e) ....

f) ....

g) ....

h) ....

i) ....

B Jack and the Beanstalk

Narrative technique is the term given to the point of view taken by the person who is telling the story.

1 From whose point of view has this story been told?

a) "I sold the cow and have this bag of beans instead of money."

.... tells the story.

b) "Jack came home with a bag of beans instead of the money."

.... tells the story.

c) Jack felt anxious about showing his mother the beans. He knew she would be angry. Jack's mother stood on the step, troubled thoughts flicking through her mind as she saw Jack approaching.

....

.... tells the story.

C Match Up

1 Match the writing viewpoint with its description by joining them with an arrow.

First-person narrative	gives an objective view of the action and main characters but is not one of the characters.
Second-person narrative	sees into each character's mind and follows the action wherever it is.
Omniscient third person	Is told of the action.
Third-person narrative	is told by the person involved. Mentions 'I'.

2a) Write two or three sentences about your favourite activity from your own point of view.

....

....

....

....

b) Write two or three sentences about your friend's favourite activity from your point of view. [✓ Checkpoint in answers]

....

....

....

....

8 First-Person Narrative

When one character tells the story and uses the personal pronoun 'I' this is writing in the first person. Words such as 'my' and 'our' are possessive adjectives and may be included in first-person narrative writing.

A Turn About

Writing in the first person places the reader as the immediate receiver of what the character is saying.

Example:

"All day I tramped. I am sure I was on the right track but it was difficult and almost impossible to pick up any trail markings so I decided to stay put and wait until someone found me."

1 Complete each sentence using first-person pronouns and possessive adjectives.

a) The day began early as .... had to be at the airport three hours before .... flight.

b) On the way to the airport .... discovered .... had left .... flight bag at the hotel.

c) It was obvious the taxi-driver was not pleased with .... and he u-turned sharply to show his displeasure.

d) As soon as we arrived at the hotel .... leapt out and hurried to recover .... bag.

B Flying's For the Birds

1 Circle all the personal pronouns and possessive adjectives in the following paragraph.

I do not like flying, especially the takeoff. It is stressful waiting for the plane's wheels to lift off and I always find myself gripping the seat arms tightly with my knuckles showing white. It always amazes me to find I have been holding my breath and, once the land drops smoothly away below, I release it with a thankful sigh. It takes a little more time for me to release the grip I have on the armrests but eventually, once the nerves stop jangling, I manage to unlock my fingers.

C Me, Myself and I

1 Write a paragraph in the first person where you are telling of an event that has made you feel emotional in some way. Write striking first and last sentences.

....

....

....

....

....

....

D I Remember When ...

1 Write about an incident you were involved in that made you, and perhaps others, laugh uncontrollably and that you now remember with pleasure. [✓ Checkpoint in answers] ....

....

....

....

....

....

Second-Person Writing

Writing in the second person uses the pronoun 'you' to indicate that this is the person being spoken to.

A Life's a Beach

Writing in the second person places the reader on the edge of what is happening to the characters.

Example:

Terry turned to Ian and said, "You have been patient but you will have to wait a bit longer. It is not like you to be so impatient, so please wait until the end of the week and you will find everything will be fine."

1 Complete each sentence by using a pronoun from the box.

you	I	she	her	they

a) Yesterday I saw .... at the beach and .... thought

.... looked really cool on your new surfboard.

b) Was that your cousin who was with ....?

.... looked very nice and so did .... family.

c) Do .... come to the beach often?

.... would like to meet .... sometime.

B Surf's Up

1 Circle different pronouns that indicate that this paragraph is written in the second person.

"You are amazing when you're riding your surfboard. I saw you outside the last breaker waiting for a big one. It was awesome when you caught it and I watched you ride it like a pro. Where did you learn those moves? They were fabulous! How long have you been surfing? Do you compete in competitions? Sorry, don't mean to be nosey, but you have impressed me and I'm blown away by your talent. You're awesome! You catch them so well. Wish I had your skill! Could we surf together next weekend?"

C You Are Awesome!

1 You probably have someone you know well who has a skill you find awesome. Write a paragraph in the second person as if you were speaking to that person about their abilities. [✓ Checkpoint in answers]

....

....

....

....

....

D Change About

1 Change the following passage from first-person narrative to second-person narrative.

My horse, Kit, always stood quietly while he waited for me. I have seen him turn his head in my direction and toss his mane and stamp his feet while I chatted with friends. He was the most patient animal and obviously thought I was wonderful. I was lucky to have had such a quiet and gentle friend.

....

....

....

....

....

10 Third-Person Narrative

When relating a story in the third person, pronouns such as he, she, they, them, it, are used. The reader is aware of one main character but others are included in the writing. The writer does not reveal all the characters' thoughts, feelings or motives to the reader.

A Uncle Colin

1 Place suitable pronouns and possessive adjectives in this piece of writing to indicate it is written in the third person.

Uncle Colin, my mother's oldest brother, lived and worked on the family farm. .... was a nutbrown man, with skin stretched over .... bony frame which never seemed to tire although .... left the house at first light and came back after dark. Thick, black, curly hair was kept neatly trimmed and, regardless of the weather, it was never out of place. Yet it was .... eyes that were .... most dominant feature, shiny brown and filled with warmth and kindness. Although .... appeared to be stern and unbending it was .... eyes that gave .... away. Try as .... might, the twinkle in .... eye was always .... undoing.

B Ski Expert

1 Circle the pronouns that show that this paragraph is written in the third person.

Swish! The gentle sound of the snow spraying in a tail from under the blades followed the skier as he cut down the mountainside. Dressed in black, he looked like a bird as he swooped and curved through the spectators. They stopped to watch him as he continued defying the slope. Confident and at ease with himself, he skied smoothly, driving the sticks into the snow time and again, until finally, with unmatched grace, he disappeared around a curve.

2 Write two sentences about someone taking part in an event. Be sure to write it in the third person.

C Twist the Tale

1 Relate a fairy tale or legend in the third person, but give a twist of your own to the ending. Be imaginative and have fun!

[✓ Checkpoint in answers]

The All-Seeing Eye

The 'All-Seeing Eye' is also called the 'Eye of God' technique. This is because the writer relates the inner lives of the characters - their thoughts, emotions, reactions to situations and their relationships with others.
Writing from this point of view uses the same pronouns as writing in the third person.

A From Different Perspectives

1 What three people could possibly be involved in the following incidents? Choose people whose perspective you could use to write about the incident.

a) A bike and a car collide.

- ❑ ....
- ❑ ....
- ❑ ....

b) A swimmer has to be rescued.

- ❑ ....
- ❑ ....
- ❑ ....

c) A skier breaks a leg.

- ❑ ....
- ❑ ....
- ❑ ....

d) A rugby player sustains an injury.

- ❑ ....
- ❑ ....
- ❑ ....

B Take an Incident

Each character can be given equal importance and the reader learns how an event may have a different effect on each participant.

1 Choose one of the incidents in A and write brief notes of how that incident is seen through each of those involved. Note their thoughts, feelings, reactions. [✓ Checkpoint in answers]

The incident chosen from A is:

❑ ....

❑ ....

❑ ....

C Pursued by Fear

1 Explain in your own words how the writer has used the 'Eye of God' technique here. Quote from the passage to illustrate your explanation.

Shirley ran like the wind ahead of the others, her heart pounding as her feet hit the road in a drum-like beat. Her sister Frankie, brow wrinkled with anxious thoughts, ran almost at her heels, while far behind, her short legs pumping madly and breath aching as it left her lungs, struggled Laura. Not one of them wanted to stop until they had reached somewhere safe.

....

Tone

Tone is the author's attitude to the subject being written or spoken about. In conversation the meaning is conveyed by voice tone as well as by the words themselves. Writers convey their attitudes and feelings to the reader in the way they write.

A Cool It

Tone is the attitude of a piece of writing.

Examples:
Impolite: "What are you snivelling for, you whimp?"
Polite: "Why are you crying?"

1 Rewrite each of the following sentences so that the tone is polite and reasonable.

a) "You've stuffed up all my work."

....

....

b) "That computer is useless. It's as slow as a wet week."

....

....

c) "I'm not picking that rubbish up. No way. It's not mine."

....

....

d) "That's cool. Really choice. Wish I could go on a trip too."

....

....

e) "Maths is the pits. I'm really dumb when it comes to algebra."

....

....

B Write That Again

Rewrite this paragraph so that the tone is more formal.

"Look, I don't know who you think you are but I'm sick of you spreading lies about me. If you don't stop now I will make sure everyone knows what a liar you are."

....

....

....

....

....

....

C Simply Sort

Sort these words into the chart below according to whether these attitudes are favourable or unfavourable in tone.

Supportive, Encouraging, Conceited, Miserly, Insipid, Aggressive, Unpretentious, Sincere, Arrogant, Conscientious

Favourable	Unfavourable
....	....
....	....
....	....
....	....
....	....

D The Day is Gonna Rock!

1 Rewrite the following paragraph in a more formal tone. Change the slang, colloquialisms and abbreviations.

'There's heaps of snow, no crowds, and this baby's got it all, from sweet clear runs to gullies, bowls and big rollers - the day is gonna rock! Hang on a mo! Whether you're a first-timer or experienced and a cool downhill skier, take time out to think safe - mountain safe.'

....

....

....

....

Setting 13

The time and the place of a piece of creative writing is the setting. Clues to the time that events occur and the place in which they occur are given by the writer. From these clues the reader is able to understand more clearly what the writer is trying to convey.

A Knowing the Time

1 What time in the history of New Zealand would be conveyed by these sentences?

a) 'The old man crouched behind the flax bush and watched as a large canoe with square mats on poles sailed into the bay.'

The time in New Zealand history would be:

....

b) 'Men left their farms to be run by their wives and children and volunteered for "The Great Adventure".'

The time in New Zealand history would be:

....

c) 'The neighbours arrived in full force, squeezed into the lounge and sat silently staring at the box.'

The time in New Zealand history would be:

....

B Knowing the Place

1 Write an interesting opening sentence for a creative writing piece on each of the following places.

a) Beach ....

....

....

b) Wharf ....

....

....

c) Skatebowl ....

....

....

d) Bush ....

....

....

e) Dentist's room ....

....

....

C Adding Detail

1 Using the five senses helps the writing become clear and colourful.
Fill in each block with notes that relate to one of the topics in B.

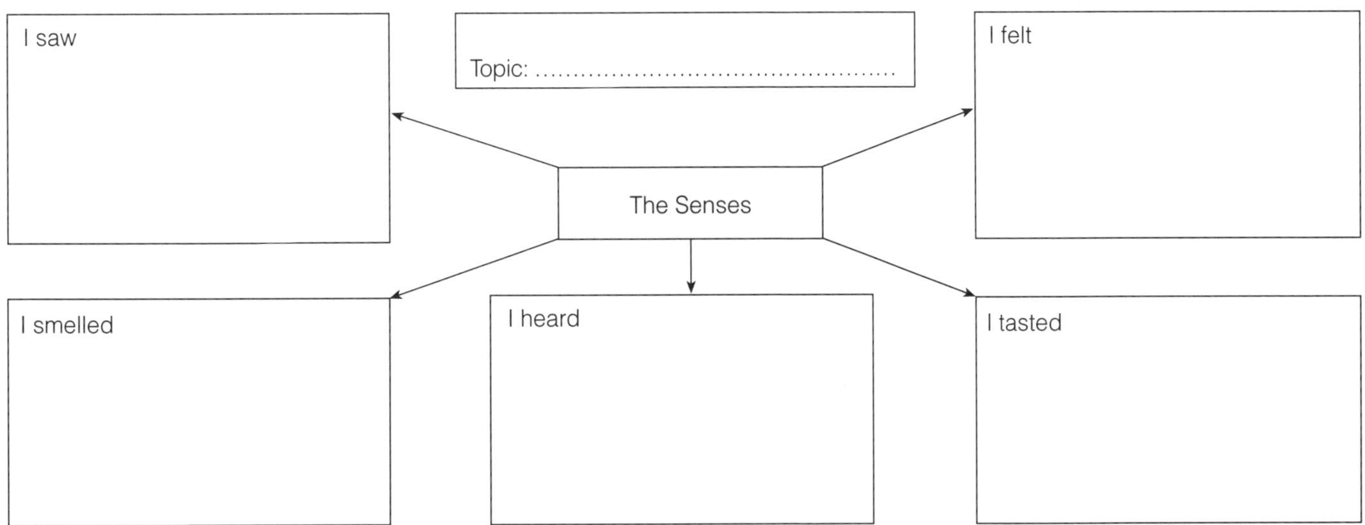

14 Character

AS 1.1
Writing

A character in a story is presented to the reader through a physical description as well as by what the person says, thinks or does and by what others have to say about them. All these aspects contribute to a mental picture of that person.

A Building a Character

1 Circle the words that create an unpleasant character.

a)

amiable
sarcastic
gracious
spiteful
sympathetic
intimidating
overbearing
obliging
affectionate
cunning

b) The words that remain indicate a person who is

.... in character.

B Get the Picture

1 For each of the following people, list four words that would be useful to build a character description.

Arrogant Person	
Spoilt Child	
Concerned Parent	
Fussy Person	

C Two Sides to a Character

1 By selecting precise words, very different characters may be written about. In these two basic paragraphs, develop two widely different characters by placing appropriate words in the spaces.

a) Tom sat .... The cliff ahead looked .... to him and he was .... he could find the .... to begin. He had always felt .... about heights. With legs that felt .... he stood and walked .... towards the cliff base.

b) Tom sat .... The cliff ahead looked .... to him and he was .... he could find the .... to begin. He had always felt .... about heights. With legs that felt .... he stood and walked .... towards the cliff base.

2 Show that you are able to develop different characters using the same method. Underline the words that show the differences.

a) ....

....

....

....

....

....

....

b) ....

....

....

....

....

....

....

D Amazing Adjectives

1 Descriptive words, or adjectives, add interest and detail to writing. Adjectives help create a picture in the mind of the reader. Underline the adjectives in this example of descriptive writing.

Peter sat cross-legged on a large cushion which lay on the bare wooden floor. He wore long, baggy, black pants and a thin white shirt, opened at the front, through which could be seen a bony rib-cage and a thin sprinkle of fine black hair covering his chest. It was obvious he hadn't shaved for some days as his whiskers were quite long. He didn't notice anyone as he was lost in his own world.

Stereotypes 15

A stereotype is an image or idea of a particular type of person or thing that has become fixed through being widely held. The main character in any writing or text should never be a stereotype.

A What a Character

Stereotypical characters usually show only one side.
Good: brave, courageous, innocent
Bad: scheming, cruel, immoral

Examples: Cinderella: innocent, hard-working, kind
Stepsisters: cruel, lazy, spiteful

1 Within the school environment there are students and teachers who are categorised as stereotypes. For each of the following write words or phrases that show how their appearance is often mentally visualised.

a) The clever student:

....

....

....

b) A team captain:

....

....

....

c) The Drama teacher:

....

....

....

2 How do you see these characters? Write brief notes.

a) Rugby player: ....

....

....

b) Multisport athlete: ....

....

....

c) Lawyer: ....

....

....

B Good Guys vs Bad Guys

1 Using sources such as popular magazines, cut out or draw pictures which could be placed in each of the following categories.

a) Bad Guys

What signals show a bad guy?

....

....

....

....

....

....

b) Good Guys

What signals show a good guy?

....

....

....

....

....

....

16 Events

AS 1.1
Writing

When writing about events, it is important that the events take place in chronological order (in order of time). The sequence of events must unfold as they happened rather than the writer skipping forward and back in time.

A It's My Life

1 Write one important event in each of these years of your life.

Age	Event
5	
6	
7	
8	
9	
10	
11	
12	
13	
14	
15	

B Surf's Up

1 Rewrite these events in the logical chronological order.

a) Select a place and unpack the car.
b) Lifeguards give shark warning.
c) Return to water activities.
d) Change for a swim.
e) Swimmers and surfers leave water.
f) Pack the car.
g) Wait for 'All clear'.
h) Repack car to drive home.
i) Drive to the beach.
j) Surf the waves.

....

....

....

....

....

....

....

....

....

....

C Mountain Peak Rescue

1 Write a sequence of story ideas about these events.

A	B	C

Picture A ....

....

Picture B ....

....

Picture C ....

....

Sentence Length 17

Good writing should be simple, clear and concise. The sentences should vary in length to give variety to the writing, as the continual use of short sentences becomes boring. The words used should clearly express what has to be said and show knowledge, understanding and a command of language.

A Improving Quality

Sentences need to vary in length to eliminate boredom.

Example:

Logan had a new blue sweatshirt. He thought he looked choice.
This could be improved by:
Logan, a thirteen year old, had been given a dark blue sweatshirt for his birthday. He thought he looked choice.

Adding adjectives is a way to increase sentence length.

1 Improve the quality and length of these sentences by adding adjectives. Circle the adjectives.

a) The car skidded across the road.

....

....

b) I picked up the surfboard and ran down the beach to the waves.

....

....

c) High in the sky, a bird glided.

....

....

d) Sarah brushed her hair in front of the mirror.

....

....

e) Tom clambered over the rocks to the entrance of the cave.

....

....

B Just Your Best Ideas

1 Complete these sentences varying length and complexity.

a) The frail old man ....

....

....

b) She was torn from sleep ....

....

....

c) Hemi crouched ....

....

....

d) Like a bullet. [✓ Checkpoint in answers] ....

....

....

e) With eyes glittering ....

....

....

C The Bungee Rocket

1 In the following paragraph there are six sentences but the full stops and capital letters have been omitted. Proof-read the paragraph and replace the omitted punctuation. Use a red pen and write over the top of the printed words.

As you take your seat harness and belt up you know this is no ordinary amusement ride your mind races and your throat begins to dry while your heart rate increases dramatically you wait the countdown begins without further warning you are slingshot skyward in a reclining position at 160 kph facial muscles are stretched and distorted by the g's

18 Dialogue

Dialogue is conversation. Any dialogue used in writing supports or adds to what has taken place. All dialogue is indicated by the use of speech marks at the start and end of the words spoken.

A "And I Said"

Punctuation indicates the spoken word or dialogue.

Example:

The wind whispered through the leaves as the moon hid behind a cloud. "I'm frightened," stammered Julie.
"You know there's no need for that. I'll look after you, so don't be scared," James replied heartily.

1 Use speech marks and other punctuation around the direct speech.

a) Where is my bag asked Marie.

b) I've no idea replied her mother.

c) I put it by the door returned Marie and someone has moved it

d) Don't look at me, I've enough to do her mother responded.

e) Marie frowned Perhaps I've made a mistake

B A Big One

Don't give characters long speeches and only use direct speech if you are confident you know the rules and can apply them.

1 Punctuate the following dialogue.

By cripes Wiremu thats a big eel Where were you fishing asked James

Down at the big pool south of the bridge replied Wiremu

Say thats a choice place Ive fished there too but never caught anything that size

Just luck Bro Just plain luck

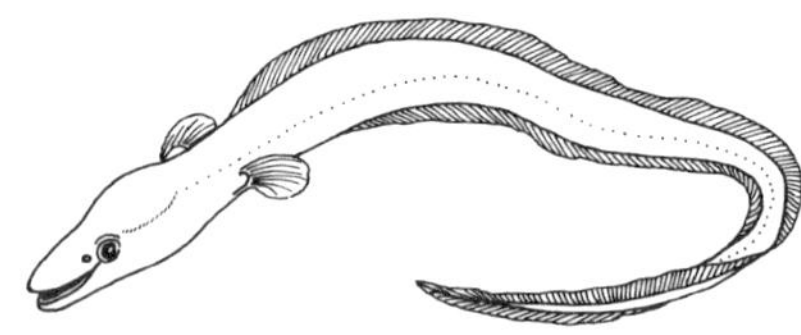

C Who's There?

1 Punctuate these "Knock, Knock" jokes for practice. Use all punctuation required.

Knock knock
Whos there
Albert
Albert who
Albert youll never guess

Knock knock
Whos there
You
You who
Did you call

Knock knock
Whos there
Ya
Ya who
Ride em cowboy

Knock knock
Whos there
Althea
Althea who
Althea later alligator

2 Explain why the punctuation marks have been used in each of these examples.

a) "Mount Taranaki is smaller than Mount Aorangi," said Hemi.

....

....

b) "It is not wise," said the Park Ranger, "to go tramping on the mountain in this weather."

....

....

Rough Drafts

Rough drafts of a story should be written on every second line to leave room for alterations and additions.
Once the topic has been decided, the best strategy is to write without pausing for 15 to 20 minutes, allowing thoughts to flow freely.

A Story Sequences

1 Quickly write four story-sequence ideas that spring to mind for each of these starters.

a) I was trapped by my feet . . .

How? ....

When? ....

Where? ....

What happened? ....

b) "What's that on your face, Bro?"

When? ....

Where? ....

Why? ....

What happened? ....

c) There was no flicker of expression in the woman's hooded eyes.

When? ....

Where? ....

Why? ....

What happened? ....

B I Feel . . .

1 Do you have a brother or sister who loves to tease or embarrass you in front of others? Think of a time when such a situation has occurred and write about it without pausing.

[✓ Checkpoint in answers]

C Draft Editing

1 To improve a rough draft, all the elements listed in this crozzle need to be applied.

Rules for this should be well understood

Always needs to be checked

Completes a sentence

Vary the length of these

Correct structure of sentences

Used to start sentences and for proper nouns

Not to be used too often

20 Beginning, Middle, End

The basic structure of an essay should have a beginning, middle and end. The beginning introduces what you are going to write about, the middle informs the reader about what has happened and the end draws the story to a close. All areas of the structure need to be of equal interest to the reader.

A Simply Structured

Here is an example of the structure of the poem "Jack and Jill".

Example:

Beginning: Jack and Jill go up the hill.
Middle: Jack falls and is injured. Jill falls as well.
End: Jack goes home as fast as he can and goes to bed

1 Complete this chart to show the simple structure of the poem "Humpty Dumpty".

a) Beginning

b) Middle

c) End

2 Choose a nursery rhyme of your own and analyse its structure.

a) Title

b) Beginning

c) Middle

d) End

B Tale Structure

1 Choose a fairy tale, myth or legend and show the structure of the tale.

a) Title of Story

b) Beginning

c) Middle

d) End

C Pairing

1 Match up the start of the sentence with the appropriate ending by drawing an arrow between the two matching halves.

a) Structure your essay	tells the story.
b) The beginning	have a central idea.
c) Sentence beginnings	with at least three parts.
d) Paragraphs	sets the scene.
e) The middle	should vary.
f) Short sentences	follow a logical order.
g) A number of sentences	quicken the pace.
h) The end	slow the pace.
i) Essays should	make a paragraph.
j) Long sentences	closes the story.

D Writing Hints

1 Use a word from the box to complete each sentence.

interest	logical
essential	chronological
variety	details

a) Events happen in .... order.

b) Use a ....of sentence length, style and structure.

c) Grab your reader's .... from the beginning.

d) Use well chosen .... in descriptions.

e) Finish the story by bringing it to a .... and interesting end.

f) Paragraphing is .... to the structure of an essay.

Beginning or Introduction

The reader of your writing is introduced to the story in the first paragraph. This sets the scene, introduces the characters and encourages them to read on and find out what happens. It must capture their interest from the start.

A How to Begin

An essay may begin with a question, a description of a person or place, a comment by someone, a memory, or other approaches.

Examples:

Who would have thought a camping trip could be so dangerous?
"Don't you dare do that! Have the sense to keep out of it".

1 Write the first sentence you could use as an introduction to an essay.

a) A question.

....

....

....

b) A description of a person.

....

....

....

c) A description of a place.

....

....

....

....

B Star Starter Ideas

1 Add to the star diagram any word associations and ideas that are triggered by the word in the centre.

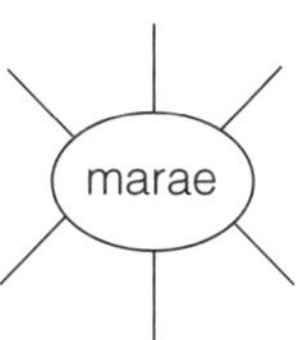

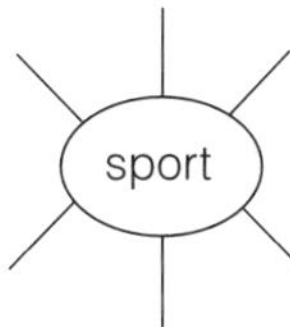

C Writing Starters

You can be given starters to write about. These can be used to write from different points of view.

Example:

I wish things were different . . .
i) Break-up of a friendship
ii) A disabled person's point of view
iii) A personal fear

1 Give three different viewpoints for each of these starters.

a) The experience had altered me . . .

i) ....

ii) ....

iii) ....

b) I watched spellbound . . .

i) ....

ii) ....

iii) ....

c) There was a sense of calm . . .

i) ....

ii) ....

iii) ....

22 Middle or Body

The introduction of your essay writing is followed by the middle or body. This is a series of paragraphs that link and continue the development of the events that happen or the conflict that arises and the people who are involved. They include descriptive words that give colour and life to the writing. The interest provided by the writer in the first paragraph must continue.

A Body Hints

1 Match the start of the sentence with the appropriate ending by drawing an arrow. These sentences are useful hints on writing the body of an essay. One is done for you.

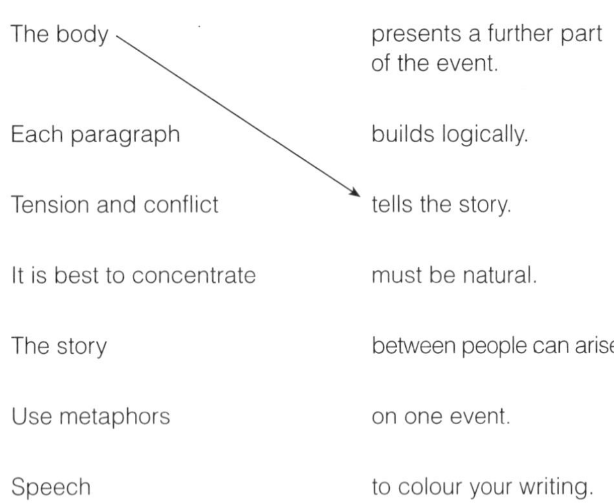

The body	presents a further part of the event.
Each paragraph	builds logically.
Tension and conflict	tells the story.
It is best to concentrate	must be natural.
The story	between people can arise.
Use metaphors	on one event.
Speech	to colour your writing.

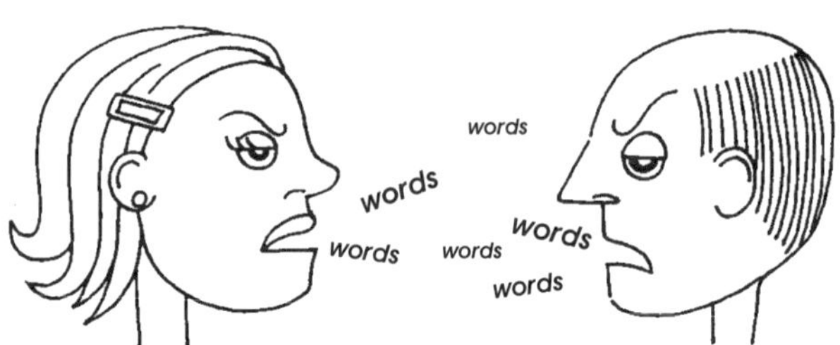

B I Told You

1 Think of a disagreement you have recently had with someone. Note briefly these points:

a) How it began. (Introduction)

....

....

b) How the conflict continued. (Body)

....

....

....

....

c) What the climax of the disagreement was. [✓ Checkpoint in answers]

....

....

2 Write eight adverbs that could be used to help create tension when writing about the event. One is done for you.

.... **aggressively** ....

....

....

....

C Simple Story Structure

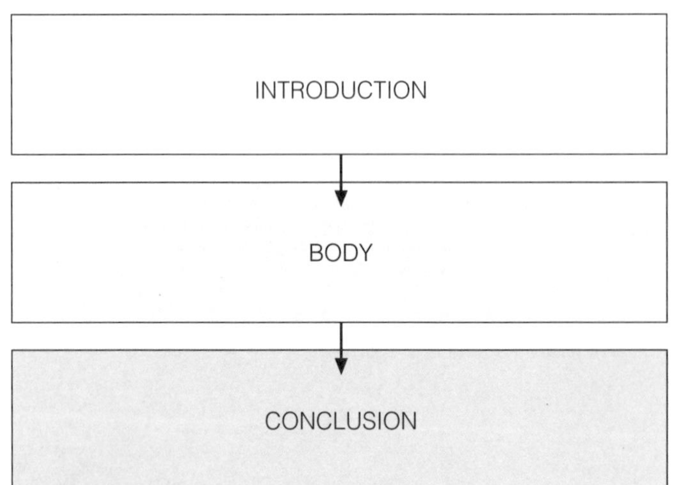

Introductory Paragraph
Introduces the setting and perhaps some of the people in the story. "Sets the scene".

The Body
Tells the main part of the story. Tells what it is all about: the What, When, Why, How, Where. Each paragraph presents a part of the story but they must link together.

Conclusion
Finishes the story by bringing it to a conclusion which should be believable and interesting.

End or Conclusion 23

The reader wants the story to end in a way that satisfies or surprises and is convincing. As much impact is required in the conclusion as in the introduction. It must be believable. Stories should never fizzle out!

A Sticky Situations

1 For each situation that follows, write two possible interesting conclusions.

a) Your first attempt at driving a car.

i) ....

....

ii) ....

....

b) A movie date arranged by a parent without your knowledge.

i) ....

....

ii) ....

....

c) A friend has listened to gossip about you and has been influenced by it. You thought they were a loyal friend.

i) ....

....

ii) ....

....

d) You have been grounded for a month by your parents for what you consider a small misdemeanour.

i) ....

....

ii) ....

....

e) You have decided you need to be far more active and have chosen skateboarding as a possibility to improve fitness.

i) ....

....

ii) ....

....

B Subject Scenarios

1 What do you think were the subjects of the essays that used these sentences as part of the concluding paragraph?

a) *No birds were in sight, only the twisted trees, lifting their blackened arms to the sky, signalling for help.*

The essay was about ....

b) *"You caught the first wave - just like that! You can ride 'em!" "Oh! That was nothing really. Just a bit of luck," she replied.*

The essay was about ....

c) *Try as he might to give the appearance that he was strict and uncompromising, to those who knew him well, the twinkle in his eye was always his undoing.*

The essay was about ....

d) *The sun filtered through the canopy, with golden fingers touching the fallen leaves that lay curled and layered on the bush floor. Peace and tranquillity prevailed, disturbed only by bird-song and the flutter of wings.*

The essay was about ....

C Rescue!

1 This picture shows a tense moment. What could the climax be? Write a brief synopsis of the conclusion.

[✓ Checkpoint in answers] ....

....

....

....

....

....

....

24 Achievement Standard 1.1 - Test

In this activity you will develop a piece of writing of 300 words, where you will write about a person you know well and show how he/she reveals a side of their personality or character you have not met before. Your readers are other students. [✓ Checkpoint in answers]

You will be assessed on:

- ✓ how well you express and develop your ideas
- ✓ how well you organise your material
- ✓ your ability to use a writing style appropriate to the task
- ✓ your accuracy in spelling, punctuation and paragraphing

You may need to continue your answer on refill.

What to Write About

It is important to select a topic you have some knowledge about, care about, or have some interest in. Lack of knowledge can be easily recognised by the reader because the opinions or arguments lack depth.

A Issues for Students

1 Topics may be issues at school. Name five topics that could be of interest to students.

a) ....
b) ....
c) ....
d) ....
e) ....

2 Name five topics that could be of interest to teenagers outside of school.

a) ....
b) ....
c) ....
d) ....
e) ....

B At Home and Abroad

1 Topics may be of local interest. Name five topics of general interest to people in your local area.

a) ....
b) ....
c) ....
d) ....
e) ....

2 Name five topics of national interest to New Zealanders.

a) ....
b) ....
c) ....
d) ....
e) ....

C In My Opinion

1 You have been asked to select three topics, different from those in A or B, suitable for a formal essay in each of the following categories. Make sure you have some knowledge and opinions on the issues you have selected before writing down the topic.

School Issues

a) ....
b) ....
c) ....

[Local organisations, the school newspaper and teen magazines may be good resources]

National Issues

a) ....
b) ....
c) ....

[Local and national newspapers may present ideas]

Global Issues

a) ....
b) ....
c) ....

[National newspapers, television news bulletins and TV documentaries will provide information]

26 Gathering Information

AS 1.2
Planning

It is important, early in the year, to gather information on issues that arise in school, in the local area, or are of national importance as well as those that are of international interest. Such information gathering will be relevant to your research assignment.

A On the Brain

1 Brainstorm as many sources of information you could possibly find to be of use in each of these areas.

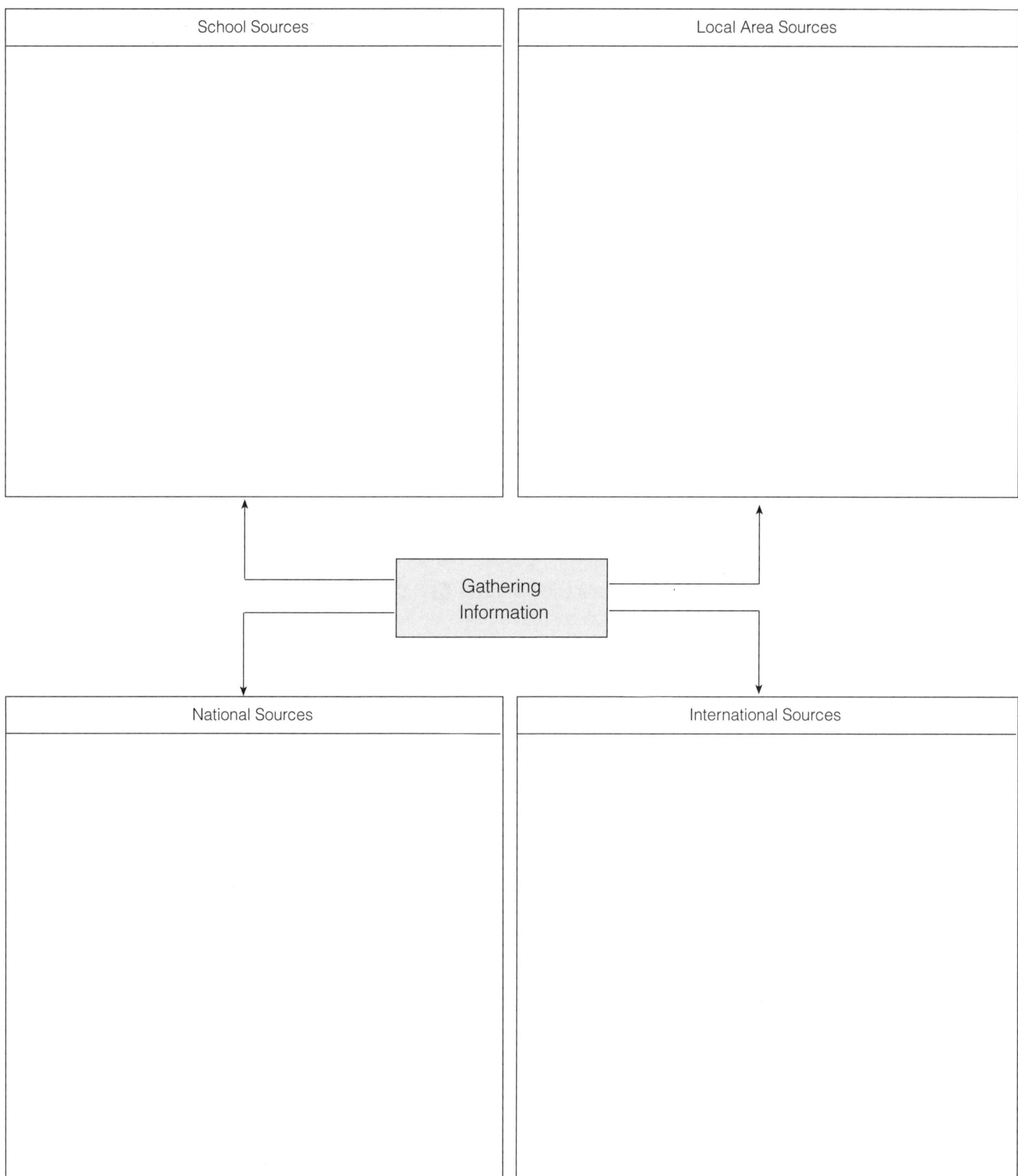

Brainstorming

To construct a good argument or to present an opinion on a topic in formal writing, the first process is to brainstorm and map out what is already known. From this brainstorming, three or four ideas which support your opinion become the basis of the writing.

A Our Heritage

1 Brainstorm the following topic for a formal writing exercise.

Topic: Preserving our Natural Heritage

B Give Your Opinion

Select three or four ideas on a given topic.

Example: Bullying in Schools.

a) The problem is both in and out of school.
b) Who the bullies are.
c) Who the victims are.
d) Constructive steps to deal with the issue.

1 Write three or four ideas on each topic to form the basis of a formal essay.

a) School Uniforms.

❑ ……………………………………………………………………
❑ ……………………………………………………………………
❑ ……………………………………………………………………
❑ ……………………………………………………………………

b) Homework.

❑ ……………………………………………………………………
❑ ……………………………………………………………………
❑ ……………………………………………………………………
❑ ……………………………………………………………………

C Positive and Negative

A possible plan of attack to organise the brainstorm material is to sort the ideas into positive and negative aspects of the issue.

1 From the notes you have brainstormed on the topic of 'Preserving our Natural Heritage', place the ideas on the appropriate sides of this chart. [✓ Checkpoint in answers]

Positive Aspects	Negative Aspects

28 Essay Planning

When planning an essay, the material that has been brainstormed needs to be organised in a logical way, so that the opinion or argument will be clearly stated and supported.

A Positive Points

1 In each of the following issues tick (✓) the idea that supports the viewpoint and put a line through the negative idea.

a) Bullying in Schools

- ❖ Inform those in the school support system.
- ❖ Ignore getting involved.
- ❖ Use of teen mediators.
- ❖ School - a safe environment.
- ❖ Talk to someone.

b) Teens Take Responsibility

- ❖ Being 'cool' is the most important thing.
- ❖ Contributing to the family by working.
- ❖ Supporting fellow teens.
- ❖ Working as volunteers.
- ❖ Involved teens are successful teens.

B Logical Order

1 In your considered opinion list the positive ideas for the two topics in Exercise A. Place them in the best order for writing a formal essay.

a) Bullying in Schools

- ❖ ....
- ❖ ....
- ❖ ....
- ❖ ....

b) Teens Take Responsibility

- ❖ ....
- ❖ ....
- ❖ ....
- ❖ ....

C Two Plans

1 Choose two topics that interest you as a basis for formal writing and write a brief paragraph plan of three or four points you wish to develop.
[✓ Checkpoint in answers]

a) Topic :

1.
2.
3.
4.

b) Topic :

1.
2.
3.
4.

Paragraphing 29

Each paragraph in formal writing deals with one main point. Each point is presented in a structured way and this formula makes writing simple. The S.E.X. formula indicates: Statement, Explanation, eXample. There are other acronyms to describe the formula but the structure is the same.

A Fallen Forests

1 Label this exercise with the S.E.X. to indicate the order in which they should be arranged in a paragraph.

a) Half the world's rainforests have been destroyed since World War II.

b) Deforestation is a dangerous threat to the world of the future.

c) Destruction of forests at an alarming rate occurs mainly in areas between the Tropics of Cancer and Capricorn.

2 The natural resources of our coastline are being destroyed by people taking more than their limit.
Plan a paragraph which develops this idea.

a) Statement ....

b) Explanation ....

c) Example ....

B Plan a Paragraph

1 You are to choose a topic of your own. Write it in this box.

2 Plan a brief outline of four points you wish to make on this topic.

a) ....

b) ....

c) ....

d) ....

3 Choose one of these points and write a paragraph that clearly follows the Statement, Explanation, eXample formula.

[✓ Checkpoint in answers] ....

30 Sentence Construction

A sentence must be complete and grammatically correct. It must have a subject (the person or thing that does the action is named) and a verb (the action that happens is written). Without a verb a sentence does not make complete sense.

A Sea Creature

1 Circle the subject and underline the verb that shows the action of the subject.

Example :
a) Several herons perched on the old wharf piles
b) With mane flowing in the wind the black horse ran.

a) Sea anemones capture passing prey.

b) Most anemones remain in one place.

c) Wandering anemones move about.

d) Mangroves, rock pools, boulders and reefs provide the habitats for anemones.

e) The tentacles bristle with barbs.

2 Complete these sentences by adding to the subject given.

a) Species of anemone ....

....

b) Paralysing barbs ....

....

c) Passing victims ....

....

d) Small sea creatures ....

....

B Amazing Anemones

1 These sentences are poorly constructed in some way. Explain why they are not correct.

a) Anemones eat shrimps because they are there.

....

....

b) Anemones which live in the sea environment are different.

....

....

....

c) The anemone is neither fish or shellfish.

....

....

d) The variety of colour in anemones makes them look like a garden.

....

....

....

e) Victims wait to be killed by anemones that cross their path.

....

....

....

C In Agreement

1 The subject and verb must agree in sentences. Place one of the words in the list at the start of each sentence. Use each word once. Make sure that there is agreement between verb and subject.

a) .... there been any shrimps in the pool?

b) .... the anemone opened its tentacles?

c) .... there a fish in the pool?

d) .... there many anemones?

e) .... there small fish as well as shrimps in the pool?

f) .... the anemone pink or purple?

Is
Are
Was
Were
Has
Have

Introductory Paragraphs

The introductory paragraph in formal writing establishes the topic that the essay is about, the main points to be covered and the angle or point of view from which it is to be written. Grabbing the attention of a reader from the very beginning is important.

A Which Approach?

1 Write a good opening sentence for an essay on 'Examinations - a necessary evil', using the following techniques.

a) A question:

....

....

b) Your own opinion:

....

....

c) A general opinion:

....

....

d) An unusual beginning:

....

....

B Writers' Rules

1 What rules have you learnt about formal writing? Write a rule about each of the following that would be worthwhile as a hint to writers.

a) Point of View: ....

....

....

b) Level of Language: ....

....

....

c) Sentence Structure: ....

....

....

d) Opening Sentence: ....

....

....

C Formally Identified

1 Identify the examples of formal language by placing [F] in the appropriate box and informal language by recording [I] .

a)	Education's for the birds.	[ ]	f)	Disruptive behaviour is not acceptable.	[ ]
b)	Education is the key to success.	[ ]	g)	Take advantage of your educational opportunities.	[ ]
c)	Homework is an essential part of student life.	[ ]	h)	Nothing is ever achieved without enthusiasm.	[ ]
d)	Homework? Who does that?	[ ]	i)	Always put your best foot forward.	[ ]
e)	Behave properly. Don't be a pest.	[ ]	j)	Set goals for yourself and go for it.	[ ]

2 Choose one of the examples in C that you identified as formal and write three or four sentences for an opening paragraph on that topic. Make sure you continue in the same tone. [✓ Checkpoint in answers]

....

....

....

....

....

....

32 Body of the Essay

In formal writing, the body of the essay is the most important part and has three or four main points that present the view of the writer. Each paragraph deals with one point following the S.E.X. structure previously covered on Page 29. When writing the body, present the weakest point first and the strongest point last to create the impression of a strong argument overall.

A What Ideas I Have!

1 Write four ideas that could be developed as an argument on the advantages of wearing school uniforms.

a) ....

b) ....

c) ....

d) ....

2 Write four ideas that could be developed on the advantages of not having to wear school uniforms.

a) ....

b) ....

c) ....

d) ....

B Clearing Up Conventions

1 Unscramble these words that refer to the conventions you must keep in mind when writing.

a n g l l s e p i

....

b) t t u u p c a i n n o

....

c) r r a a m m g

....

d) n n e e e s t c   r r u u t t s e c

....

e) p p a a a g g r r i h n

....

C The Editor Writes

1 Editorials in newspapers aim to influence by logical argument. There are often several well-thought-out ideas backed up by reason and examples. Using an editorial from a newspaper, complete the following chart.

Topic of Editorial:

	Main ideas Point 1	Point 2	Point 3
Main ideas			
Reasons/examples			
Editor's opinion			

Conclusion

The conclusion of an essay should sum up the issue presented and leave the reader with a thought-provoking statement. There should be some link back to the introduction and so this is the place for possible solutions to the issue. The introduction, body and conclusion of a piece of formal writing should present a strong case and leave the reader with something to think about.

A Overused and Obsolete

1 Formal writing should avoid cliches or overused phrases such as "At this moment in time...", or "The issue at hand...", or "All credit to..." Write six overused phrases or cliches you have heard.

a) ....

....

b) ....

....

c) ....

....

d) ....

....

e) ....

....

f) ....

....

B Wildlife Preservation

The conclusion is not the place to introduce any further ideas, as the end rounds off issues already presented in the previous paragraphs.

1 Complete this concluding paragraph on the preservation of wildlife with a thought-provoking sentence.

Each New Zealander should be aware that the preservation of all wildlife is of the utmost importance to future generations. The dwindling in numbers of kiwi, kokako and kakapo is due to predators who have endangered their future. The decimation of shellfish on the New Zealand shoreline by those more interested in profit than preservation is of grave concern. Even the natural forest, once widely spread, is now confined to specific areas ....

....

....

....

....

....

....

C Paua Poaching

1 In a newspaper article on the poaching of paua the following points were mentioned:

- ❑ Paua resources are being decimated by poaching and are not recovering.
- ❑ Legal-sized paua are already difficult to find in some areas.
- ❑ Black marketeers buy paua at high prices because of scarcity.
- ❑ Hundreds of thousands of paua are sent overseas each year.

Write a concluding paragraph in formal style that sums up these points and concludes with something for the reader to think about.

[✓ Checkpoint in answers] ....

....

....

....

....

....

....

....

34 Formal Diction

Formal writing must have formal language. Slang, colloquialisms, abbreviations and unacceptable words have no place in formal writing.

A Sticky Situations

1 Rewrite the following informal language in more formal terms.

a) I'm really brassed off.

....

b) She keeps stirring things up.

....

c) He has done a bunk.

....

d) He's a pain in the butt.

....

e) She is a waste of space.

....

B A Chip Off The Old Block

1 Rewrite the following paragraph in formal style.

John was carried away at the thought of a holiday with his dad as he was a chip off the old block. They both enjoyed hunting in the bush, even when it rained cats and dogs, and they seldom got into hot water. His dad had taught him to respect the bush and not act the goat, otherwise he could sink or swim on his past experience.

....

....

....

....

....

....

....

....

....

....

C Figure It Out

1 Figurative language is acceptable in formal essays as it can enhance the writing. In each box write some examples of figurative language. [✓ Checkpoint in answers]

Similes - Example : Karen ran as swift as a deer through the bush.
a) ....
b) ....
c) ....

Metaphors - Example : Karen floundered through the mud.
a) ....
b) ....
c) ....

Personification - Example : Grunting and groaning, the tractor pulled the tree trunk.
a) ....
b) ....
c) ....

Syntax is the arrangement of words to create well-formed sentences. Essays should include compound and complex sentences to connect ideas.

A Making Sense

1 Rearrange the words in each box to make a well-formed sentence.

a)

the	and	was	meat	skins	to
introduced	New Zealand		rabbit		for

....

....

b)

originally	trout	from
rainbow	California	came

....

....

c)

stoats	predators	native	are
weasels	on	and	wildlife

....

....

d)

orchards	opossums	damage
gardens	forests	and

....

....

B Making Clear

A compound sentence is made up of two or more simple sentences of equal weight joined by a co-ordinating conjunction.
Examples : and, but, then, either + or.

1 Write two compound sentences and circle the co-ordinating conjunctions used.

a) ....

....

....

b) ....

....

....

A complex sentence is made up of two or more simple sentences joined by a subordinating conjunction.
Examples : as, lest, although, since, because, if, unless.

2 Write two complex sentences and circle the subordinating conjunctions used.

a) ....

....

....

b) ....

....

....

C In My Opinion

1 Label each sentence either simple, complex or compound. There are two of each.

a) The myna is a bird from India.

b) Because rabbits have overrun farmland, they must be exterminated.

c) The English hare was introduced for sport and it is still hunted today.

d) The stoat and the weasel are predators.

e) The hedgehog controls garden pests, but it may eat eggs as well.

f) The Red Deer is the most common species because it was the earliest to be introduced from England.

Signposts

Signposts in formal writing are the key words that show that the argument is being developed in a logical sequence. They connect one paragraph to the next.

A Showing the Bones

1 For each of the topics given, write 'signposts' for two paragraphs that show the development of the argument.

a) Te Reo Maori/Maori language and its importance.

❐ *"It is important for any culture to retain their language heritage because . . . ."*

❐ ....

b) Water Safety.

❐ ....

❐ ....

c) Peer Pressure.

❐ ....

❐ ....

B Clever Comparisons

In presenting an argument it is useful to develop a point that you have made by including comparisons.

1 Include each word or phrase in the box in a sentence that shows a comparison being made.

a) however	b) although
c) similarly	d) on the other hand

a) ....

b) ....

c) ....

d) ....

C Supporting the Statement

1 Choose one of the topics in A and select the first of the 'signposts' that would be most suitable for presenting the first argument. Remember, the statement you make on this point must be supported by an explanation and an example.

Topic Chosen:

Signposts for argument:

The first argument must have: A statement, an explanation and an example. Compose the first argument on the lines below.

[✓ Checkpoint in answers] ....

Rough Drafts 37

A rough draft is the first attempt by a writer to explain their ideas on a topic.

A Teen Talk

1 Choose one of the topics and write a short article, formal in tone, for a student newspaper. [✓ Checkpoint in answers]

* Being involved is being smart.
* Tolerance - an important quality.
* Fashion trends.
* The family that plays together, stays together.

You may need to continue on refill.

B Review and Refine

Even the best writers have rough drafts. It is impossible to construct a well-written essay without some review.

1 Using the short article written in A, check off the following criteria.

	Criteria	Yes	No	Sort of
a)	There are paragraphs.			
b)	The topic is stated in the first paragraph.			
c)	Each sentence is well constructed.			
d)	There is no slang or colloquialism.			
e)	Ideas are clearly stated.			
f)	Ideas follow a logical order.			
g)	What is written is interesting.			
h)	All spelling is correct.			
i)	Punctuation has been used correctly.			
j)	Each sentence begins differently.			
k)	It is formal in tone throughout.			

C Monitoring Me

1 From the criteria listed in B above, to what areas of writing do you need to pay special attention? List them here.

38 Rewriting

Having written a rough draft, there is a process for you to go through to make the writing clearer and more polished. This is the process of rewriting and it is the secret to producing quality writing.

A Polish and Perfect

1 Using the draft written on the previous page, think critically about the ideas presented then rewrite the whole piece polishing and improving each step. [✓ Checkpoint in answers]

....

You may need to continue on refill.

B Good Advice

1 Place the listed words in the spaces provided in the paragraph.

quality	regardless	achieving	revise	scribble

The secret to .... good writing is to .... a first draft .... of quality and then .... and revise until .... emerges.

C Something to Think About

1 What 'rule' would you apply when you are doing each of the following?

a) Writing the opening paragraph of the essay.

....

b) Writing the conclusion of the essay.

....

c) Proofreading the essay.

....

2 Name four good things writing should be (four words).

....

....

3 What must be kept in mind when choosing an essay topic?

....

Spelling

Spelling is learnt by understanding the formation of the word and by practice.

A Train Your Eye

1 Proof-read for spelling and underline the errors in this first-draft writing. There are eight errors.

Youth problems have become nationwide news. Stories have constantely circulated, highlighting concerns over the iresponsible behaviour of some young people. The articles have claimed that children as young as ten have had there stomachs pumped out after weekends of drinking and drug-taking. Police say the problems being caused by the young teenagers include fighting, crimminal damage, smashing bottles, litering and drunk and disorderley behaviour. It is hoped an increased police presense will be a deterrant to future misbehaviour.

2 List the correct spelling for the eight misspelt words.

....

....

....

....

....

B Short Yet Clear

Mistakes are often made when writing because of the misuse of some words.

1 Write a short sentence to show your clear understanding of the use of each of the following. [✓ Checkpoint in answers for e) and f)]

a) practice ....

....

b) practise ....

....

c) beat ....

....

d) bet ....

....

e) affect ....

....

f) effect ....

....

C The Kiwi Way

1 Label each box with ***N.Z.*** if the word is spelt that way in New Zealand, or ***U.S.*** if it is American spelling. Write the New Zealand spelling beside the American.

a)	program	
b)	aeroplane	
c)	centre	
d)	analyze	
e)	colour	
f)	jail	
g)	traveler	
h)	cheque	
i)	aluminum	

D Tuhituhi e Hoa

1 Write the Maori for each of the following. The first letter is given to you.

	English	Maori
a)	abalone	***p*** ....
b)	sweet potato	***k*** ....
c)	chief	***r*** ....
d)	old woman	***k*** ....
e)	red	***w*** ....
f)	Sunday	***R*** ....
g)	wood pigeon	***k*** ....
h)	house	***w*** ....
i)	fish	***i*** ....

40 Punctuation

AS 1.2
Editing

To write well and to make what is written clearly understood, it is necessary to have a comprehensive understanding of punctuation.

A Perfect Punctuation

1 Write a brief rule for on the use of each of the following.

a) Full Stop

b) Comma

c) Semicolon

d) Colon

e) Question Mark

f) Exclamation Mark

g) Apostrophe of Possession

h) Apostrophe of Omission

i) Inverted Commas

j) Brackets

B Excuses, Excuses

1 Edit the following passage for punctuation.

Teenagers are forever giving excuses it appears that the moment they enter those teen years a whole set of different rules applies these rules relate to doing homework making beds keeping their room tidy or eating proper meals every request is responded to with varying excuses that stretch the patience of parents teenagers who would want them

C Who Said That?

Speech marks (" ", ' ') are used around the words that are spoken.

Example: "Where are you going?" Tom asked.
"Nowhere," replied Theresa.

Both double and single speech marks are acceptable.

1 Use speech marks around the words that are spoken in each of the following.

a) Sarah has gone to the movies, said Sarah's mother.

b) Who has she gone with? asked Emma.

c) I think she was meeting Paul, replied Sarah's mother.

d) Do you think she would mind if I met them there? queried Emma.

e) No. I'm sure that would be fine.

f) I'll catch a bus into town, said Emma.

g) Look, Sarah's mother declared. I'm just going into town now so I can give you a lift.

h) That's great. Thanks.

Grammar 41

Grammar is the whole system and structure of language, consisting of the arrangement of words and phrases to create well-formed sentences. It includes the way a change in a word makes a change in its meaning.

A Changing Tense

To write in a tense means to write in the past, present or future.

Example: Past: I have eaten my kai / I ate my kai.
Present: I am eating my kai / I eat my kai.
Future: I will eat my kai.

1 Rewrite each sentence and change to past tense.

a) The sun shines brightly.

....

b) High in the tree, birds are singing.

....

c) In the distance a dog is barking.

....

d) The car is coughing and spluttering.

....

e) I worry long and hard about the problem.

....

f) I stand, without moving, holding my breath.

....

g) I will take my car when I go to the South Island.

....

B Making Changes

Words may change from one part of speech to another by the addition of a prefix or suffix.

Example: port (noun)
export (verb)
portable (adjective)

1 Form a verb from these nouns by adding a prefix.

a) earth .... b) judge ....
c) value .... d) mask ....
e) hand .... f) arm ....
g) test .... h) govern ....
i) lock .... j) burden ....

2 Form an adjective from these nouns by adding a suffix.

a) earth .... b) judge ....
c) value .... d) mask ....
e) hand .... f) arm ....
g) test .... h) govern ....
i) lock .... j) burden ....

3 Use prefixes and suffixes to make verbs and adjectives.

Noun	Verb	Adjective
seal		
cross		
forest		
trust		
feat		

C Correct Choice

1 Choose the correct word from the bracket and write it in the space.

a) I am not .... to drive as I am too young. (legible, eligible)

b) It is ....the way he behaves. (contemptible, contemptuous)

c) Dog owners must have a .... (licence, license)

d) I enjoy steamed pudding as a .... (desert, dessert)

e) He..................................his opponents to the finishing line. (beat, bet)

f) The All Blacks went on .... to France. (tore, tour)

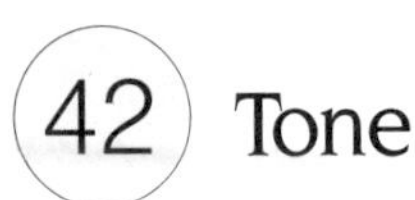

42 Tone

Tone is the author's attitude toward the subject. A serious tone should dominate in formal writing.

A Into Columns

1 Sort these words into the two columns according to the tone implied. There will be five in each column.

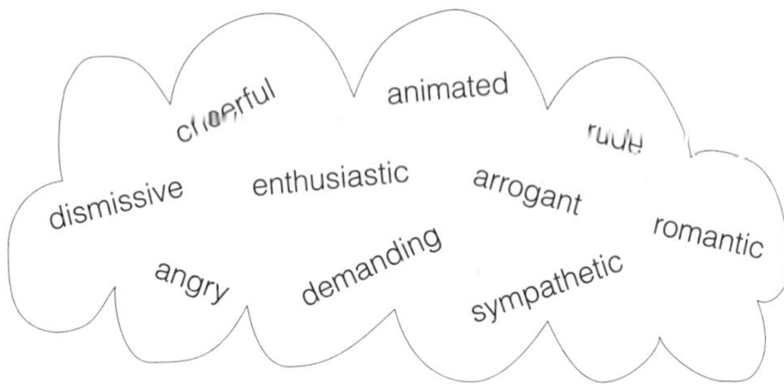

Positive Tone	Negative Tone

B Seriously Said

calmly	spitefully	sympathetically	seriously
excitedly	tartly	anxiously	gleefully

1 What word would suit each of the following sentences to convey the tone?

a) "Ladies and gentlemen, it is my pleasure to welcome you here," said the chairperson ....

b) "She thinks she is perfect but she's such a snob," said Amy ....

c) "Look! I can do it!" shouted Peter ....

d) "I think you must sit down and wait for the decision," said the coach ....

e) "I'm sure you don't need to worry. Wait until we have more news," said Leanne's mother ....

f) "I've got the biggest present," shouted Hone....................

g) "Look, I'm going first if you can't make up your mind," responded April ....

h) "Don't you think we are on the right track?" asked Henry ....

C Tone

1 In the wordfind there are eighteen words that indicate tone. Look in all directions to find them, then list them in the two columns. (There is no order required in the columns).

....	....
....	....
....	....
....	....
....	....
....	....
....	....
....	....
....	....

T	R	I	U	M	P	H	A	N	T	L	O
N	L	I	U	Q	N	A	R	T	H	C	K
A	B	U	S	I	V	E	I	N	O	E	A
Y	S	U	R	L	Y	T	H	G	U	A	H
O	O	G	N	I	T	A	O	L	G	R	L
U	F	L	L	U	F	E	P	O	H	N	U
B	T	L	D	I	S	M	A	L	T	E	F
D	I	S	T	A	N	T	M	D	F	S	Y
E	V	I	S	N	E	P	L	I	U	T	O
R	S	E	R	E	N	E	A	E	L	C	J
T	I	O	S	U	O	I	C	I	L	A	M

Appropriate Language

Language must suit the subject and the audience.

A Keep it Simple

1 Write a simpler word beside each of the following words.

a) indigenous ....

b) optimal ....

c) facilitate ....

d) component ....

e) indicate ....

f) parameters ....

g) utilize ....

h) viable ....

2 Place the words in the appropriate places in these sentences.

members	profession	specialized
indispensable		context

Jargon is a .... language used among .... of a trade, ... or group. Jargon is .... to those who use it in the .... of their work.

B Simply Said

1 Rewrite the following sentence in language that is less wordy.

a) The neighbours had just bought a pre-owned automobile.

....

....

b) Because of company restructuring Peter had been made redundant.

....

....

c) During systematic inquires it was discovered that the factory was accountable for a chemical spillage.

....

....

d) The military personnel made a strategic withdrawal.

....

....

C Correct Choice

1 Complete this chart with a definition and an example for each of the following kinds of language.

Language Use	Definition	Example
a) Cliche		
b) Slang		
c) Euphemism		
d) Idiom		

44 Redundant Words

Redundant words are those that are able to be omitted without loss of meaning.

A Get it Right

1 Rewrite these sentences, eliminating the unnecessary words.

a) We must co-operate together.

....

b) The factory was in close proximity to the river.

....

....

c) When travelling, it is important to take the basic essentials.

....

....

d) It is a true fact that New Zealanders have a highly competitive spirit.

....

....

e) The audience at the play first began to squirm in their seats.

....

....

B Get Rid of Them

1 Cross out the unnecessary words but make sure the sense is retained. Some words may be added.

a) The patient in the end room is a mentally ill patient.

b) A dedicated teacher helps each student to become a better student both academically and emotionally.

c) His skill in carving was absolutely unique and stood alone in the field of carving.

d) Her complexion became pink in colour as she was teased by her friends.

e) Boys today wear clothes that are invariably too large in size.

f) Nick hurriedly scribbled a quick note to his mother on an envelope.

g) Those on the dole are often described or stereotyped as all lazy.

h) Samuel still hasn't gone to the dentist yet.

i) Karen was determined in her mind that she would lose weight.

C Simplify What is Said

1 Write one word for the underlined phrase in each sentence.

a) At this point in time we must continue to be strong.

b) We must return to the nearest hut due to the fact that the weather has deteriorated.

c) Make sure that everyone knows exactly what to do for the purpose of safety.

d) In spite of the fact that the weather is bad it will not take long to go back.

e) It is important, in the final analysis, that all trampers keep together.

f) In order to make safety a priority the slowest will go first.

g) The dress was along the lines of a medieval gown.

h) The lotto win was in the neighbourhood of three million dollars.

i) We will be going on holiday before you know it.

j) All credit to the All Blacks for their efforts today.

Assessment Standard 1.2 - Test

Choose ONE of the topics listed:

- Families are the core of society
- Teenagers are terrific
- Advertising, the manipulator
- Raising the drinking age is a must
- Equality for all
- The insidious influence of peer pressure

Present a written argument which explores this topic. You can present more than one viewpoint or develop one particular point of view. Your writing will appear on a page featuring young people's views in a local newspaper. Ideas you include should be explained and supported by examples. You should write at least 250 words.

You may need to continue your answer on refill.

Plot

The plot consists of a situation which leads to a conflict or problem between characters. This leads in turn to a climax or crisis, after which the problem is sorted out and a resolution made.

A Plotting the Plot

1 Circle the type of extended written text you are studying then list the main events of the work in chronological order. Give the title of the text and name the writer.

a) Text type: Novel Hyperfiction Play

b) Title of Text: :

c) Writer:

d)

Main Events That Occur in Text

B Vital Moment

1 Identify one or two climaxes in the text. Explain what led up to this moment, who was involved and what the resolution was.

[✓ Checkpoint in answers]

Sub-plot

A text may have a sub-plot running alongside the main plot. This adds depth and complexity to the story. The sub-plot generally involves minor characters yet interweaves them with major events.

A Plot and Sub-plot

1 Writing brief notes only, complete this chart.

a) Title of text :	
b) Author :	

c) Complete this chart. If there is no sub-plot in your text, leave the second section blank.

Structure of The Main Plot	
How and where the story begins	
Conflicts between characters in text	
Crisis point or climax in text	
Resolution of conflict	
Structure of The Sub-plot	
How and where the sub-plot begins	
Conflicts that arise in the sub-plot	
Crisis point or climax in sub-plot	
Resolution of conflict in sub-plot	

d) If your text has a sub-plot, explain how it parallels the main plot and how it emphasises the ideas or themes. [✓ Checkpoint in answers]

....

....

....

....

....

Theme

The theme is the most important consideration in the story. It is the ideas, issues or message the writer wants the reader to consider. The theme is rarely stated. It is through the events, the interaction of the characters, what is said, reactions made to situations, the climax and its resolution that the reader receives the writer's message.

A Thinking of Themes

1 For each of the themes in the list, name a novel, film, play or TV show which has that theme. State the category it belongs to e.g. film, TV show.

a) Good versus evil ....

b) Triumphs and troubles of friendship ....

c) True love triumphs ....

d) The horror of war ....

e) Coping with dramatic change ....

f) Trials of growing up ....

B Message Received

1 Using an incident in the text being studied show how that incident conveys a message from the writer to the reader.

Incident →	Characters Involved →	What Happened →

Why it Happened →	Reactions by Character →	Climax of Incident →

Resolution to Incident →	Writer's Message →	Reader's Response

Major Characters

There are generally only one or two major characters in an extended text. An understanding of a character is built up by what they do, what they say and think, and how they interact with others as well as what others say about them.

A Character Profile

1 Brainstorm a profile of two major characters in the text being studied using the following aspects to help build that profile.

physical appearance — attitude
relationships — character

a) Title of text: ....

b) Writer: ....

c) Character One : ....

....

....

....

....

....

d) Character Two : ....

....

....

....

....

....

B Character Analysis

1 Choose one of the characters in A and answer the following questions. [✓ Checkpoint in answers for a)]

a) What is your personal impression of them?

....

....

....

....

....

....

....

....

b) Why does this character have the respect/disrespect of others?

....

....

....

....

....

....

....

....

C Relating to Others

1 How does the major character in B relate to minor characters? Write the name of the major character here :

	Name	How the major character relates to this minor character
a) Minor Character No.1		
b) Minor Character No.2		
c) Minor Character No.3		
d) Minor Character No.4		

50 Minor Characters

Minor characters are those who are not so involved in the plot but make a contribution in some way.

A Personal Profile

1 Draw or find a picture of a face that looks like a minor character in the text being studied. Write brief notes covering his/her qualities, traits, personality, appearance and relationships with others.

a) Title of Text: ....

b) Writer: ....

c)

Character :	Personal Profile :

B Someone I Know

When reading we can see in characters the traits of people we know and we respond to those characters in the way we respond to real people.

1 Choose a character from the text who has traits similar to a person known to you. Explain what it is about this person that you respond to and why. Give examples and detail from the text to support what you write. [✓ Bullet point in answers]

a) Title of text: ....

b) Writer: ....

c) Character chosen: ....

....

....

....

....

....

....

....

....

....

C Favourite Character

1 In the text being studied who is a favourite character? He / she may be a major or minor character. Write brief notes, under the following headings, about this character and what he / she is like.

a) Title of Text: .... b) Writer: ....

c) Character chosen: ....

d) What is this character like physically? (Tall, short, old etc.). ....

....

e) Does this character represent anything else? (Innocence, greed, spite etc.). ....

....

f) Is the character stereotyped in any way? (Fat = lazy, athletic = hero etc.). ....

....

g) How does the character change during the course of the story? ....

....

....

Setting

The setting refers to the place/s, the time covered, the era (which can be the past, present or future), and the social background or environment in which the characters live.

A Thinking Carefully

1 Using a text being studied, write one or two well-constructed sentences, supported by details and examples from the text, about each of the following.

a) A place described in the setting : ....

b) Era in time: ....

c) Social background or environment: ....

B Outside Influences

1 From the text being studied, describe why the setting is important to the story as a whole. How does the setting influence the way the characters behave or think?

[✓ Checkpoint in answers]

C Clearly Descriptive

1 Draw a sketch of a place that has been carefully described in the text being studied, or construct a picture from magazine clippings, then select phrases from the text that the author has used to describe the place. Quotations like these are ideal 'specific details' required in the mark schedules for literature standards.

Phrases from the text.

52 Social Background

The social background or environment from which the characters come affects the way they behave.

A Upstairs and Downstairs

1 Sort the information given into the appropriate column.

takes orders	well educated
frugal	few rights
gives orders	extravagant
household uniform	little education
controlling	well dressed

Upstairs	Downstairs
Gentleman	Servant
....	....
....	....
....	....
....	....
....	....

2 Classes of Society - Circle the words that indicate a person who speaks in a socially acceptable manner.

agreeable sullen restrained provincial mild boasting modulated blustering judicious brash

B Basic Behaviour

1 List three or four ways of behaving you could expect from these people which are due to their environment. Do not repeat words.

a) Caveman:

....

....

b) Nurse:

....

....

c) Maori Warrior:

....

....

d) Spoilt Child:

....

....

C Diverse Characters

1 From the text being studied write some of the clues given to you about two different characters.

a) Title of text : .... Author : ....

b)

Character No. 1	Name :
Social background	
Environment	
Qualities of Character	

c)

Character No. 2	Name :
Social background	
Environment	
Qualities of Character	

Style 53

Style is the way in which an author writes. The writing may be simple and down-to-earth or complicated and abstract.

A Message Received

The way the author writes conveys to the reader certain messages.

Examples:

'The whanau met at the beach every Sunday.'
This conveys to the reader the story is set in New Zealand.

'I feel that you are imposing on my hospitality.'
This is spoken in a formal manner by an educated person.

1 What does the writer convey in each of these examples?

a) *"Here, mate, get your swanni on an' we'll head for the bush."*

....

....

b) *"Without further ado, I declare this meeting closed."*

....

....

c) *'Not daring to breathe, Angela crouched, trying to melt into the ground, as the flashlight, like an evil eye, searched for her."*

....

....

d) *With eyes shining with glee, the whole group burst into raucous laughter as Paula walked slowly away.*

....

....

B Decisive and Significant

1 From a text being studied, write the most decisive remark made by a character and then explain why this remark is significant.

a) Title of Text: ....

b) Writer: ....

c) Character: ....

d) Decisive remark: ....

....

....

....

....

....

e) Why this remark is significant: ....

....

....

....

....

....

....

C Speaking Figuratively

1 From a text being studied, find an example of each of the following figures of speech and place it in the chart. The example does not have to come from spoken words.

a) Title of Text: .... b) Writer: ....

Metaphor	Simile	Personification
Pun	**Hyperbole**	**Irony**

54 Writing a Response

When writing a response to an extended written text question it is important to follow the S.E.X. formula: statement, explanation, example;

A And So To Begin

1 Referring to the text being studied, write the opening paragraph for an essay on one of these choices.

- This non-fiction book is worth reading
- How one character is influenced by another
- The story is true-to-life
- The story has changed my thinking

The introductory paragraph must include the title of the book, the author's name and the key words from the question you have chosen as well as a general statement.

a) Title: ....

b) Author: ....

c) Choice made: ....

....

d) Key words: ....

....

....

e) Opening paragraph: ....

....

....

....

....

....

....

....

....

....

....

....

....

....

....

B Supporting Statements

Each statement made in the body of the response - and there should be at least three - must have an explanation and an example to support the statement.

1 Make three statements relevant to the choice made in A and support each with an explanation and an example.
[✔ Checkpoint in answers]

a) Statement ....

....

Explanation ....

....

....

Example ....

....

....

b) Statement ....

....

Explanation ....

....

....

Example ....

....

....

c) Statement ....

....

Explanation ....

....

....

Example ....

....

....

Type 55

Non-fiction is literature that is true. It is about people, places and events that are real.

A Scrambled Types

1 Unscramble the following letters and list some of the types of non-fiction books there are.

a) i g r p y b o a h ....

b) a m n a u l ....

c) r v l t a e ....

d) v n t r d a e u e ....

e) i d r a y ....

f) a o i g h u b o t r p a y ....

g) s h o y t i r ....

WAY TO GO!

B Define Clearly

1 Write a definition of your own for each of the non-fiction types you unscrambled in A.

a) ....

b) ....

c) ....

d) ....

e) ....

f) ....

g) ....

C A Character Revealed

1 Complete using a non-fiction book you're studying.

a) The title of the non-fiction book is: ....

b) The author is: ....

c) Type of non-fiction: ....

d) It is about: ....

e) Describe an incident (in about 100 words) that the leading character is involved in which reveals his/her character.

[✓ Checkpoint in answers] ....

56 Viewpoint

Viewpoint refers to the way the author writes the information. Autobiographies are written in the first person. They use 'I'. Biographies are told in the third person, using 'he' or 'she' but may also contain first person through the use of quotes from interviews or letters.

A Through Whose Eyes?

1 From what point of view is the non-fiction book you are studying written? Tick the box or boxes that apply.

a) From a historian's ☐

b) From a researcher's ☐

c) From an expert's ☐

d) From an observer's ☐

e) From a scientist's ☐

f) From a character's ☐

B Special and Significant

1 Explain why you found the non-fiction text being studied special. Support your answer with reasons.

a) Title: ....

b) Author: ....

c) Explanation ....

....

....

....

....

....

....

....

....

C Retelling a Tale

1 Rewrite the following in first-person narrative.

Sarah sat on a bench at a park. She was watching two children playing on a slide. Suddenly one of the children fell off the ladder of the slide and she ran to help as there were no adults around supervising the children.

....

....

....

....

2a) Write a short paragraph in the first person. ....

....

....

....

....

b) Rewrite paragraph a) in the third person. ....

....

....

....

....

Features of Drama

The features of drama include the type of play, the viewpoint taken, the style of the spoken language for each character, the setting, plot, characters and technical features used.

A The Play's the Thing

1 Write a brief definition for each of these types of drama.

	Type	Definition
a)	Comedy	
b)	Tragedy	
c)	Comedy of Manners	
d)	Mystery	
e)	Social Comment	
f)	Farce	
g)	Melodrama	

B Join the Dots

1 Draw a line from each drama term to its definition.

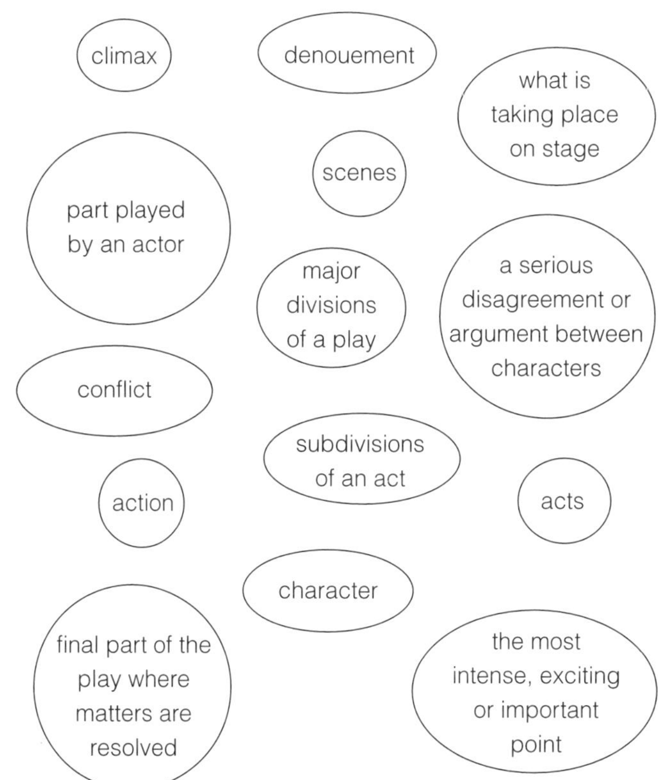

C Plotting the Plot Line

1 Use the plot line to mark with a dot the position of each event that takes place in the text being studied. State briefly what takes place in each of these events that lead to the climax and denouement.

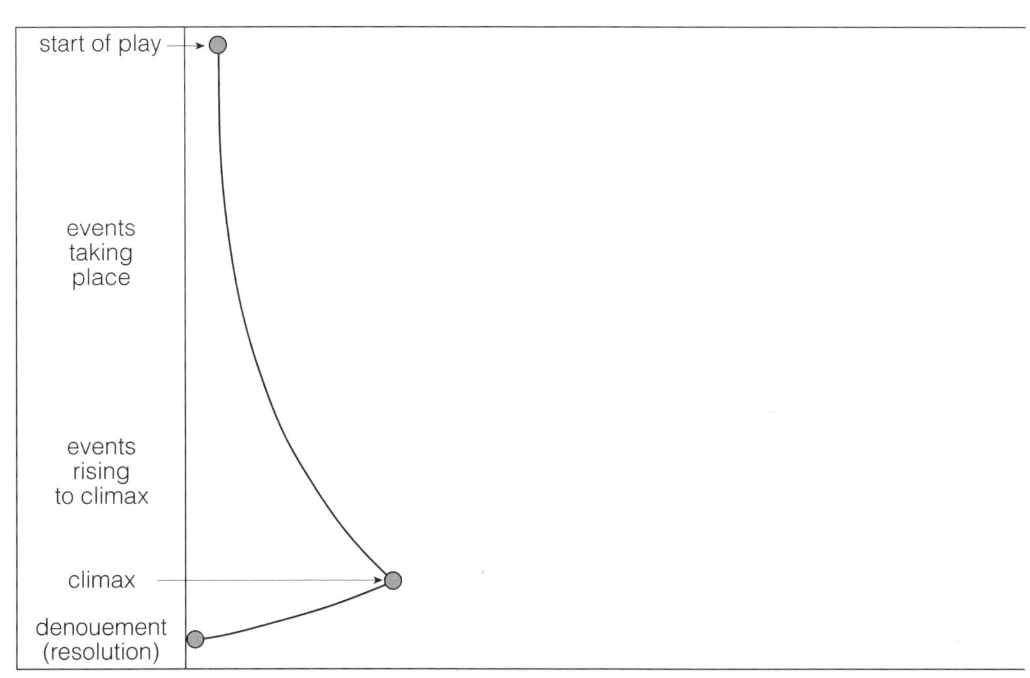

A You, The Director

1 You are to direct a play for junior secondary school students and the script that follows is the opening of the first scene. Make notes and sketches around the script of any important instructions you want to be carried out by the set designer and wardrobe designer as well as for lighting, music, props, actors' placement on stage and how you want the lines said.

Princess Perfect

Act 1, Scene 1

Throne Room in the palace of the Kingdom of Lollipop.
King is pacing up and down. Hands behind back. Worried frown. Pauses now and again. Thinks he has an idea, pauses, shakes head, resumes pacing.

Female voice offstage.

Voice : Your Majesty? Your Majesty? Has anyone seen my husband? Your Majesty? Your Majesty?

Queen : *(walking in)* Oh! There you are! I've been looking everywhere for you. Have you been here all the time? What are you doing? Why are you pacing up and down? Why are you looking so worried?

King : I've been thinking about our daughter Princess Perfect. She is not turning out to be the Princess Perfect her name suggests. In fact, she is always into mischief and everyone is fed up with her. Look what happened last week. She let the pigs out of the sties and it took the servants three days to find them. Then she decided to climb out the window and tore up a perfectly good sheet and tied it together to help her get to the ground. I don't know! I didn't do that when I was her age. I knew how to behave properly because I was a Prince. Your daughter has no idea how to be a Princess and I am trying to think of what can be done.

Queen : *(despairingly)* I know, I know! She makes me feel so ashamed at times. Where did we go wrong? What can we do?

Loud banging noises offstage - cymbals banging, drums beating, whistles blowing, etc.

Queen : *(startled)* Goodness me! What is all that noise? It must be stopped at once!

Conflict is the basis of a play. It may be that a character has internal conflict (within himself or herself) or the character may have external conflict (with other characters or circumstances).

A Considering Conflict

1 Using the play being studied, select the areas of conflict the main character has to face and list them below.

a) Play : ....

b) Playwright : ....

tough choices
loyalty to someone
conflict of beliefs
choices of action to take
conflict between characters
conflict with their circumstances
situations out of their control
conflict within themselves
family-based conflict
conflict with society
conflict of class
conflict of race

c) Areas of conflict ....

....

....

....

....

B Inside and Outside

In the play being studied, explain who the main character is in conflict with and why they are in conflict.

Main Character

has conflict with ↓

why they are in conflict ↓

C Twice the Conflict

1 Complete the following charts using two different moments of conflict that arose in the play being studied. [✓ Checkpoint in answers]

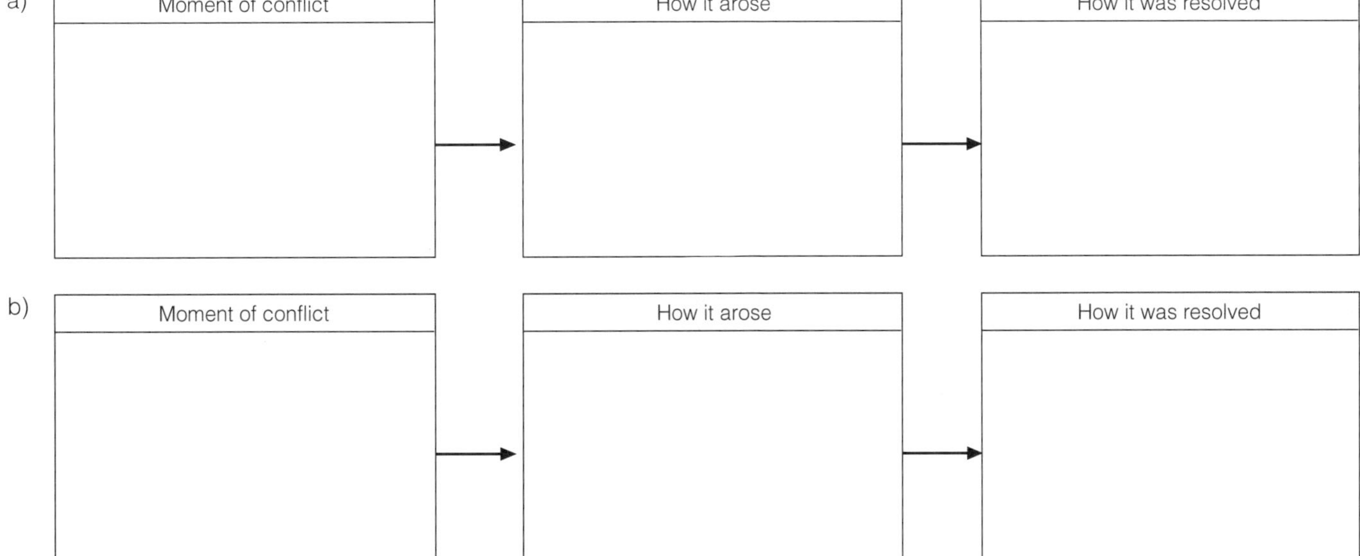

Achievement Standard 1.3 - Test

In this activity you will write about one extended written text you have studied in class. You may write about a novel, a non-fiction book, hyperfiction or a drama script. At the beginning of your answer write the text category you have selected and give the title of the text and the name of the writer.

Choose ONE question and underline it. Write about 200 words. Support your points with specific details from your text.

	1	Describe an important character in the text. Explain why he/she is important.
OR	2	What is the message the writer is conveying the reader? Explain why this message is important.
OR	3	Describe the beginning and/or ending of the text. Explain why the beginning and/or ending is important.

Title of Text : ....

Author : .... Text Type : ....

You may have to continue on refill.

Short written texts include short stories, poetry, magazine articles and short hyperfiction.

A Making Choices

1 Write the title and author of a short text being studied.

Title :	
Author :	

a) State what type of text the above belongs to (short story, poetry etc).

....

2 Tick the phrases that best suit the short written text that is being studied.

a) An incident from everyday life. ☐

b) An event and its outcome. ☐

c) A character who responds in an unexpected way to an incident. ☐

d) Feelings are revealed. ☐

e) A character who changes in some way. ☐

f) A surprising twist. ☐

g) Promotes a personal response from the reader. ☐

h) Some cultural response required from the reader. ☐

i) Involves the reader's personal experience. ☐

j) Initiates further thought on the subject. ☐

B Understanding the Text

1 Explain the relevance to the text being studied of the phrases ticked in Exercise A 2.

....

....

....

....

....

....

....

....

....

....

....

....

....

....

....

....

....

C First Impressions

1 Based on the short written text in Exercise A, answer the following question;
What was your immediate response to the text being studied and why? [✓ Checkpoint in answers]

....

....

....

....

....

....

....

....

....

Theme

The theme of a text is the idea or message the writer wants the reader to think about. It is the most important aspect of the text.

A Theme Things

The theme or idea behind a text may be summed up in a few words.

Examples:

- survival after traumatic events
- courage when faced with impossible odds
- good will eventually overcome evil
- life's adversities can be defeated with determination

1a) Write a phrase that indicates the theme of a text being studied.

....

....

b) What evidence from the text can support this theme?

....

....

....

....

....

....

B Thinking About Text

1 What does the text make you think about? Explain your thoughts. [✓ Checkpoint in answers]

....

....

....

....

....

....

....

....

....

....

....

....

....

C Three in a Row

1 Two or three texts are given for study. Write the name of each short written text being studied and the idea or message the author wants considered by the reader. One sentence should be enough.

Text No.1	Text No.2	Text No.3
Text Title	Text Title	Text Title
Author	Author	Author
Theme	Theme	Theme

Short written texts are economical in style in that only details related to the account itself are given. Each word is chosen to contribute to the effect of the text.

A Starting Style

1 Use any of the listed words to help you explain the style used in the text being studied.

formal	poetic	conversational
narrative	descriptive	persuasive

2 What is the purpose of the text being studied?

B Pictures from Words

1 Give examples of three figures of speech used in the text being studied; e.g. simile, metaphor, repetition, personification, hyperbole, alliteration.

a) Figure of Speech:

Example:

b) Figure of Speech:

Example:

c) Figure of Speech:

Example:

C Interpreting Text

1 Describe several features used in the text and explain why they are important. [✓ Checkpoint in answers]

Narrative

Some short written texts are all narrative, some mix narrative with description and / or direct comments by the author, and some may have little or no narrative at all.

A Analysing Text

1 Indicate with a ✓ in the appropriate box the phrase(s) that apply to the text being studied.

a) Text is all narrative. ☐

b) Text is a mixture of narrative with
- ❑ description
- ❑ direct comment by author ☐

c) Text has very little narrative. ☐

d) Text has no narrative. ☐

2 Indicate with a ✓ in the box the phrase that best suits the text you are studying.

a) A fiction story ☐

b) A true story ☐

c) A story told through speech e.g. an interview script ☐

d) A story told about a famous person. e.g. hero, celebrity, expert. ☐

e) A story about an ordinary person. ☐

B Quotes and Moments

1 From the text being studied answer the following.

a) Title of Text : ....

b) Writer : ....

c) Briefly describe an important moment in the text.

....

....

....

....

....

....

d) Quote a memorable sentence from the text about this moment.

....

....

....

....

....

....

....

....

C Explaining Moments

1 Write a short paragraph from one of these starters using the answers given in Exercise B. [✓ Checkpoint in answers]

- ❑ My interest in this moment was caught because . . .
- ❑ Because of this moment it was obvious that . . .
- ❑ This moment explained . . .
- ❑ A moment like this reminds me of . . .

....

....

....

....

....

....

....

....

The setting of a short written text refers to the place where the events take place, the time it is set in or the social background of the people involved. The time and place are often crucial to the circumstances and provide maximum impact, atmosphere and relevance . Often the background is sketched in quickly with details suggested rather than being specifically written about.

A Pointing the Way

The setting of a text may be anywhere the author can imagine:

* a beach on an island
* on the slopes of a volcano/mountain
* at a marae
* on a battlefield
* underground in a tunnel or cave

1 From a short written text being studied write down 3 indicators (word clues) that have given information about the setting.

Title :

Author :

Setting Indicators:

❐ ....

❐ ....

❐ ....

B Write That Again

In some short written texts the setting has some importance to events. Usually the setting is in one place.

1 From a short written text being studied give two reasons why the setting is of some importance or has an influence on what is happening. [✓ Checkpoint in answers]

Title :

Author :

a) First reason: ....

b) Second reason: ....

C Building the Story

1 Atmosphere and mood - a feeling of what it would like to be there - is very important to some short written texts. From a text being studied list the words or phrases that contribute to the atmosphere or mood.

Title :

Author :

a) Atmosphere or mood created :

b) Words or phrases used to create atmosphere or mood :

Purpose

The purpose of a text is to focus on a particular aspect of life and make the reader think in a way that may not have occurred to him/her before. Why was the text written? Was it to frighten, amuse, inform, show things from a different angle or make a point?

A Tall Tales

1 Choose either legends, fables, fairy stories or myths or a mixture of all these. Write the title and purpose for writing the story for each one.

a) Title: ....

Purpose: ....

....

....

b) Title: ....

Purpose: ....

....

....

c) Title: ....

Purpose: ....

....

....

B T.A.P.

1 What was the writer's purpose for each of the two or three texts studied? Write the title, author and purpose for each one.

a) Title: ....

Author: ....

Purpose: ....

....

b) Title: ....

Author: ....

Purpose: ....

....

c) Title: ....

Author: ....

Purpose: ....

....

C Telling Titles

1 What is the significance of the title or headline in relation to one of the short written texts being studied? Explain the reasoning behind the conclusions you have drawn. [✓ Checkpoint in answers]

Title :

Author :

....

....

....

....

....

....

....

....

....

....

Symbolism

Symbols stand for ideas. Writers may use symbols that appear throughout the text to reinforce an impression.

Examples : Here are some symbols that are easily recognised by people:
Love - A red rose, a diamond ring, a special song, a love letter.
Death - A skeleton marching across the country, the darkness of eternal night, a cross on the side of the road.

A Symbolic Ideas

1 What ideas do these symbols represent?

a) A rocky road. This represents . . .

....

....

....

b) Barbed wire. This represents . . .

....

....

....

c) A lighted candle. This represents . . .

....

....

....

B Simple Signs

1 What do you associate with the following symbols?

	Symbol	Association
a)	a kiwi	....
b)	'Rambo'	....
c)	scales	....
d)	white dove	....
e)	Red Cross	....

2 What symbol could represent each of the following?

	Symbol	Association
a)	....	blossoming romance
b)	....	a new life
c)	....	power and strength
d)	....	danger
e)	....	lack of freedom

C Symbolic Ideas

1 Using the text studied, show an understanding of an example of symbolism used and support it with details from the text. Why was this symbolism important? [✓ Checkpoint in answers]

....

....

....

....

....

....

....

....

....

....

....

Climax

The climax of a short written text comes quickly. Many texts aim to shock or surprise the reader with an unexpected twist. Some texts attempt to make the reader think further than the text itself.

A Defining Clearly

1 Using a dictionary find a suitable definition for each of the following words that could relate to a text.

	Word	Definition
a)	climax	....
b)	denouement	....
c)	resolution	....
d)	revelation	....

denouement
resolution
climax
revelation

B The End Revealed

1 From two short written texts being studied, categorise each as to whether :

- they come to an exciting climax
- matters are resolved or explained
- a problem is solved
- there is a surprising disclosure
- there is something to think about

a) Title :

Author :

Category: ....

....

b) Title :

Author :

Category: ....

....

C Think and Explain

1 Explain, by using the two short written texts being studied, whether or not the action came to a climax and how the ending made an impact on you. Show in your answer an understanding of the texts and how they relate / contrast with each other.

[✓ Checkpoint in answers] ....

....

....

....

....

....

....

....

....

....

....

You may have to complete this task on refill.

Types and Stereotypes

There are very few characters in a short written text. Many texts focus on a crisis point in the life of one character. This narrow focus increases the intensity of the story.

A Type and Stereotype

1 Using a dictionary define briefly the terms 'type' and 'stereotype' in relation to people.

a) Type : ....

....

....

....

b) Stereotype : ....

....

....

....

2 Using a dictionary define these terms used in the explanation at the top of the page.

a) Focus : ....

....

b) Intensity: ....

....

B How I See Them

1 From the short written texts being studied choose one character who is a type and note details about that person from the text which fit the type.

a) Name : [ ]

b) Supporting details : ....

....

....

....

....

....

....

....

....

....

....

....

C Character Building

1 Describe an important character from a text being studied. Explain why he/she is important. [✓ Checkpoint in answers]

....

....

....

....

....

....

....

....

....

....

....

....

70 Responding to a Text

Each reader may have a different response to a text due to personal experience.

A Responding To a Moment

1 From a short written text being studied, name a moment that made an impact on you and say why you responded to it.

B It Makes You Think

1 Using a short written text being studied, explain why it made you think beyond the text itself.

C In Response

1 From a short written text being studied write a thoughtful and perceptive response to this question, supported by examples from the text and further explanation. [✓ Checkpoint in answers]

Explain how the text made you feel and why you felt this way?

Language Features

Language features are the way words are used to achieve a particular effect.

A How Is It Spoken?

1 From the short written texts being studied write one example for each of the following.

a)	Statement:	
	What effect did this have?	
b)	Imperative	
	What effect did this have?	

B Words at Work

1 Find an example of each of the following from the text being studied.

a)	Figurative Imagery	
b)	Colloquialism	
c)	Pun	
d)	Cliche	
e)	Emotive Words	

C Effectively Worded

1 Explain how words are used in a text being studied to achieve a particular effect. Support the explanations with examples.

[✓ Checkpoint in answers]

Imagery

Imagery is figurative and descriptive language that creates a mental image.

A Senses and Imagery

1 Write the name of one of the six senses that each extract below represents.

a) *'And eat three pounds of sausages at a go
Or only bread and pickle for a week.'*

The sense represented is ....

b) *'And scarlet-flowered trees lean to drop
Their shadows on the bay below.'*

The sense represented is ....

c) *'He always liked to work the sheep close in,
Sniffing the blood, no doubt, beneath the skin.'*

The sense represented is ....

d) *'All day the shouts, cracking of leather whip,
Over bullock team and the tree's loud groan:*

The sense represented is ....

B Seeing It Clearly

1 From the text being studied, copy sentences that create a mental image for you

C Imagining Images

1 Describe two important images in each text. Explain why they are important. [✓ Checkpoint in answers]

Impact is the strong effect or influence made by what is read.

A Immediate Impact

1 Write the name of a short written text, poem, a print media or short hyperfiction example that has had an impact on you the first moment you read it.

Type of Text :

Name of Text :

Briefly explain why this example had such a strong effect on you. ....

B Clever Words

1 Impact may be created by the way language is used with an image. Draw or find an example of language working strongly with an image to create impact.

Glue your example here

C Impressions and Impact

1 Describe what had a strong impact on you in the example you chose for B. Explain why it was so effective. [✓ Checkpoint in answers]

Achievement Standard 1.4 - Test

For this exercise you must write about two short texts of the same genre you have studied in class.

The texts may have the same or different writers. You may write about :

Circle the text type you are going to write about.

- short story
- print media
- poetry
- short hyperfiction

Choose ONE of the following questions. Write about 200 words. Support your points with specific details from the two texts.

1 Describe an important idea dealt with in each text. Explain why this idea is important.

OR 2 Describe several features in each text. Explain why they are important.

OR 3 Describe several important images or details in each text. Explain why they are important.

OR 4 Describe an important character in each text. Explain why he/she is important

I have selected question number ....

Titles : ....

Writer(s) : ....

You may need to continue on refill.

Plot

The plot is the main sequence of events in a stage play, film, electronic text, television or radio production. Some indications are given as to why these events take place. Characterisation by performers, camera techniques, sound effects, lighting and music add meaning to the plot.

A Plot Parts

1 Explain briefly these parts of a plot.

a) The situation: ....

....

b) Development: ....

....

c) Climax or crisis point: ....

....

d) Resolution or denouement: ....

....

B A Plot Within a Plot

1 A visual or oral text may contain a sub-plot. What is this and what is the purpose for it?

a) A sub-plot is . . . .

....

....

....

b) The purpose is to . . . .

....

....

....

C Boxed In

1 Complete the paragraph with the words from the box.

conflict	tension
logically	dramatic
believable	audience
decisions	climax

To keep the .... interested, the plot must have .... and surprise. Each event should move smoothly forward and develop .... to make what happens .... The characters make .... the audience can relate to and dramatic events occur regularly so interest is sustained. The plot should build to a .... toward the end when the .... is at its most ....

D Perfect Plot-Line

1 Using a visual or oral text being studied, label a plot-line similar to this with the main events that occur in the production. Use a rough diagram on refill to accurately plot the events first then transfer the finished result to the space provided below.

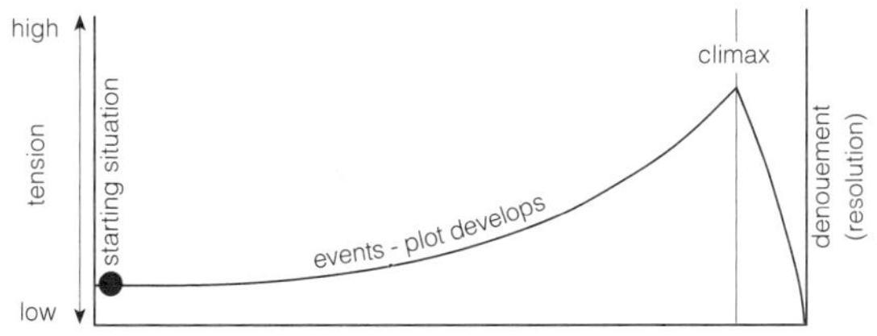

76 Major and Minor Characters

Major characters portrayed in a visual or oral text have a larger role to play than minor characters. Major characters are part of the bulk of the performance while minor characters may appear at irregular intervals. A character, particularly a major one, needs to be convincing.

A Clever Characterisation

1 Choose a major character or presenter from the visual or oral text being studied who appears convincing in his/her role.

a) Visual or Oral Text being studied:

....

b) Major character chosen:

....

c) Why this character is convincing: [✓ Checkpoint in answers]

....

....

....

....

....

....

....

....

B Minor Issues

1 From the same visual or oral text as in A choose a minor character who has an influence on a major character in some way. Explain what this influence is and how this affects what happens.

a) Minor Character chosen:

....

b) How this character has an influence on a major character:

....

....

....

....

....

....

c) How this affects what happens:

....

....

....

C Building a Character

1 Using a character from the visual or oral text being studied complete this profile. (Use note form.)

Physical details

Character chosen

....

What is known of the character's life

Personal qualities

What others say about him/her

Interaction with others

Sketch / Picture
(How I see this character)

My personal response to him/her

Text being studied

....

Set and Location

A set is a collection of scenery, stage furniture etc. used for a scene in a play or film. A location is an actual place in which a film or broadcast is made.

A Looking Carefully

1 List five things in the setting of a film which could convey information about the time, place and characters of the story to the audience.

a) ....

....

b) ....

....

c) ....

....

d) ....

....

e) ....

....

B Location, Location

1 What would be the most logical location for filming each of the following:

a) 'Devils of the Deep' ....

....

b) 'The Spanish Matador' ....

....

c) 'Desert Rats of World War II' ....

....

d) 'Hinemoa and Tutanekai' ....

....

e) 'Star Raiders 2' ....

....

C Hiding Away

1 In this wordfinder find the word that fits the definition. Circle it in the wordfinder then write it into the definition. Look in all directions. The leftover letters have a hidden message.

R	A	S	T	U	D	I	O	C	P
E	G	E	O	O	D	F	I	R	S
S	L	T	M	I	G	N	O	E	H
O	I	T	A	T	E	P	S	D	O
L	O	I	U	K	S	E	T	I	O
U	R	N	H	I	E	D	D	T	T
T	E	G	N	I	M	A	G	S	I
I	I	L	O	C	A	T	I	O	N
O	N	A	T	I	O	N	X	X	G
N	O	I	T	I	S	O	P	X	E

a) Short for properties. __ __ __ __ __

b) Place where film is shot. __ __ __

c) The __ __ __ __ __ __ __ __ is established early in a film.

d) A __ __ __ __ __ __ __ __ is an actual place.

e) One attempt at a shot. __ __ __ __

f) A large building in which interior and exterior sets can be created.

__ __ __ __ __ __

g) The __ __ __ __ __ __ __ __ __ __ is the basic information given to the audience at the start to feel involved.

h) The filming of the action. __ __ __ __ __ __ __ __

i) A list of cast, crew and those involved in making the film shown at the end. __ __ __ __ __ __ __

j) The final sorting out of the plot. __ __ __ __ __ __ __ __ __ __

The hidden message is: ....

....

78 Time

Time can be manipulated in films and television by a variety of techniques. Real time, story time and extended time are the basic time techniques.

A Time Lines

1 Match up the time technique with the correct definition by drawing a line between the two.

Real time	The film of the action is shorter than the real action.
Story time	The film of the action is longer than the real action.
Extended time	The film of the action is the same length as the real action.

B Time Clues

1 The passing of time can be shown in a film in a variety of ways. List ten possible ways this may be done.
One example is given.

a) ***A clock's hands may move on rapidly.***

b) ....

c) ....

d) ....

e) ....

f) ....

g) ....

h) ....

i) ....

j) ....

C Time and Time Again

1 Each of the techniques listed may be used in making a film or television programme.
Explain what the technique is and in what situation it could be used.

	Technique	Definition	Situation
a)	slow motion		
b)	action replay		
c)	time lapse		

Audience Appeal

A visual or oral text presents a variety of situations that amuse, excite, involve or appeal to the viewer in some way.

A Memorable Moments

1 From the text being studied list five moments that kept your attention focused on what was taking place.

a) ....

....

b) ....

....

c) ....

....

d) ....

....

e) ....

....

B Involving Feelings

1 Describe a scene that affected your feelings and explain why you felt this way. [✓ Checkpoint in answers]

....

C Who Does What?

1 Explain three ways which the visual or oral text you are studying appeals to an audience (such as humour, action, romance, conflict or tension). Give examples to support each answer.

❐ ....

❐ ....

❐ ....

80 Camera Shots

The action in a movie or TV drama is recorded using different camera shots to give variety to the viewer so they remain interested in what is happening.

A Let's Shoot!

1 The chart below covers many of the techniques used by a cameraman.
Fill in each space with the shot name and an appropriate sketch to illustrate it . Some clues are given to help you.

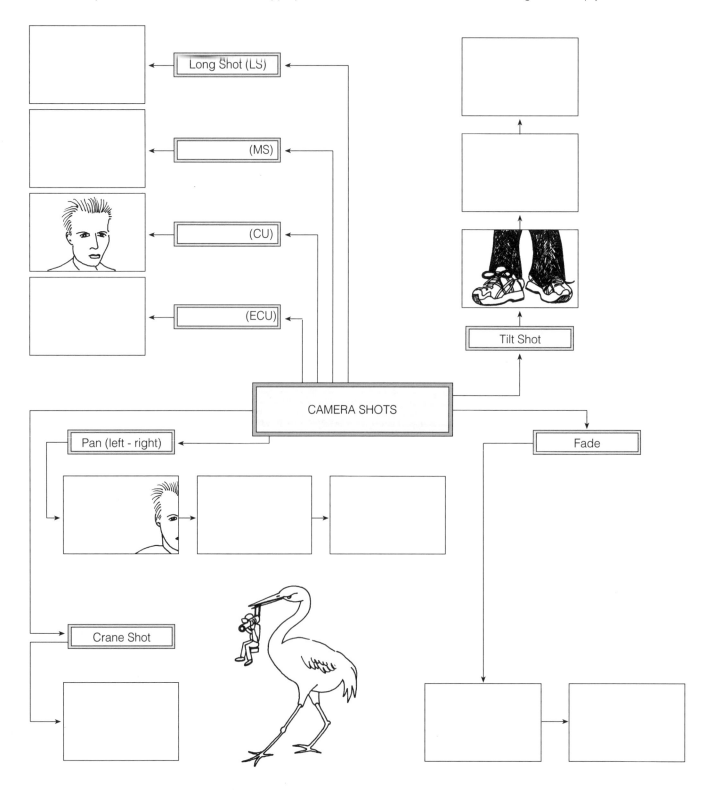

CAMERA SHOTS

Long Shot (LS)

(MS)

(CU)

(ECU)

Tilt Shot

Pan (left - right)

Fade

Crane Shot

Camera Work

Camera work enhances the action taking place by using a variety of shots, such as close-ups, to show what characters are thinking, shots to emphasise a character's reaction to a situation and unusual camera angles to create mood or atmosphere.

A Visual Impact

1 Choose one of the camera shots listed below and explain why it was used in one incident in the visual text being studied.

close-up	reaction shot
tilt shot	crane shot

a) Visual text being studied: ....

....

b) Incident from visual text: ....

....

....

....

c) Camera shot used: ....

d) Reason for using the camera shot:

....

....

....

....

....

....

B Images of Ideas

1 How has camera work emphasised ideas in one or two *scenes* in the visual text being studied?

a) Scene 1 : ....

....

....

....

....

....

....

....

b) Scene 2 : ....

....

....

....

....

....

....

....

C Cameras Roll!

1 Choose two aspects of camera work that have worked well in the visual text being studied and show how they have enhanced your appreciation of the *action* taking place. [✓ Checkpoint in answers]

❒ ....

....

....

....

....

❒ ....

....

....

....

....

82 Filming Terms

A It's a Wrap

Write the descriptions below into the appropriate boxes.

Camera angle	Cut-away	Focus
Dissolve	Establishing shot	Deep focus
Fade-in	Flashback	Freeze frame
Insert	Voice-over	Out-take
Over-the-shoulder shot	Soft focus	Reaction shot
Subjective shot	Talking heads	Tracking shot
Two-shot	Wide angle	Zoom

Descriptions :

The image may be distorted to show the character's state of mind.	A person's reaction to the previous action - nodding, surprise, terror.	A shot that turns briefly from the main action.
A detail shot. Close-up of a book page etc.	A single frame repeated many times.	A wide shot giving an overview of the scene so the action and setting is shown.
Sharpness of an image.	High angle. Low angle.	Camera moves on a dolly (platform) on wheels on tracks.
Softening the image by using filters for a romantic effect.	Often used in dialogue scenes to highlight faces.	Narration not accompanied by an image of the speaker.
Broad angle of view. Increases the sense of depth and distance.	A take not used in the final film.	A shot that smoothly moves in closer or retreats away from an object or person.
An image gradually becomes clearer.	A shot where two people are shown.	One image fades in while another fades out.
Sharp focus from foreground to background.	A return to a scene of the past.	A scene of all talk and no action.

Visual Contrast

Contrast is an obvious difference between two things placed close together. Contrast in a visual text may be shown through character, clothing, lighting, music, colour and make-up.

A Dress Code

1 From the visual text being studied choose two individuals and show how their clothing shows visual contrast and enhances their personal character.

a) Text being studied : ....

b) Character 1 : ....

c) Clothing and Character : ....

d) Character 2 : ....

e) Clothing and Character : ....

B Colour Contrast

1 Explain how contrasting colours (through lighting or costume) can influence the viewer and produce responses to characters or moments of action in a visual text.

....

C Enhancing a Moment

1 Choose one of the following to show how contrast has been used in the visual or oral text you have studied in class.

music graphics special effects dialogue properties

[✓ Checkpoint in answers]

....

Lighting

Lighting is provided by two sources. There is natural light and artificial light. Lighting may be used to highlight actors, create mood or atmosphere or show changes in time or season.

A Mood Lighting

1 Choose a scene that has worked well because of the lighting techniques used to create *mood* and *atmosphere* and explain why this has added to the effectiveness of the scene.

B In the Spotlight

1 From a text being studied choose a moment when lighting is used effectively to highlight a *character* and answer the following questions.

a) Who was the character highlighted?

b) What situation was the character involved in?

c) Why was the lighting technique effective in this situation?

[✓ Checkpoint in answers]

C Light on the Situation

1 Choose a situation where two lighting techniques have worked well in the visual text and show how they are important. Select from over-lit, under-lit, side-lit, colour filter, back-lit, etc.

	Lighting Technique Used	Importance of Lighting in the Situation
a)		
b)		

Sound is the music, background noise, sound effects and dialogue used in a visual or oral text.

A Two Sounds

1 Using details from the text being studied, choose two sound effects and explain how each of these contributed to the ambience of a scene.

Sound 1
....
....
....
....

Sound 2
....
....
....
....

B Setting the Scene

1 Outline three hints given to the audience via the dialogue at the beginning of the text that help set the scene.

❑ ....
....
....
....

❑ ....
....
....
....

❑ ....
....
....
....

C Sound It Out

1 Choose two characters who have widely differing voice qualities in the text being studied. Explain how this adds to the effective portrayal of each character. [✓ Checkpoint in answers]

a) Character : ....
Age : ....
Voice quality : ....
....
Character Portrayal : ....
....
....
....
....
....
....
....
....

b) Character : ....
Age : ....
Voice quality : ....
....
Character Portrayal : ....
....
....
....
....
....
....
....
....

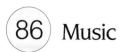

Music in productions sets the mood and helps to create tension or relaxation.

A Theme Music

1 Name some film themes that have become successful from their inclusion in a film.

a) ....

b) ....

c) ....

d) ....

e) ....

2 Music introduces certain moods into a movie. What orchestral instruments would dominate for each of these moods?

a) Romantic mood : ....

b) Melancholy mood : ....

B Sound of Music

1 List the five phrases that refer to the use of music in a film.

makes up the sound track
sets the mood
affects the emotions
signals romantic moments
builds tension
should intrude
supports the setting
composed by the conductor

a) ....

b) ....

c) ....

d) ....

e) ....

C Mood Music

1a) Using a film, TV or radio programme being studied, explain the type of music that is used to introduce the production and why that particular music has been used.

....

....

....

....

....

....

....

b) Is this introductory music repeated in the production? .... If so, when is it repeated and why?

....

....

....

....

....

....

Special Effects

Special effects are illusions created for films and television by props, lighting, camerawork, make-up, costuming, miniatures and computer-generated graphics.

A Looking Special

1 Name a recent film that has used special effects as a major part of the production and list four of those special effects.

Name of film : ....

Special effects used :

❑ ....

❑ ....

❑ ....

❑ ....

2 Name a television programme that uses special effects and list four special effects that have been used.

Programme : ....

Special effects used :

❑ ....

❑ ....

❑ ....

❑ ....

B Seeing is Believing

1 From the films and television programmes listed in A choose two different special effects and describe how they appeared on screen. [✓ Checkpoint in answers]

a) ....

....

....

....

....

....

....

b) ....

....

....

....

....

....

....

C Used for Effect

1 From the text being studied, explain the impact of one special effect that has been used and how it added to your enjoyment and understanding.

....

....

....

....

....

....

....

....

....

....

....

88 Atmosphere and Mood

Atmosphere is the pervading tone or mood. Atmosphere and mood are created by sound effects, music or voice tone.

A Hearing Images

The atmosphere or mood is introduced at the beginning by using sound effects to create a certain response.

Example:

Bird song and running water → peace and nature

Carnival music and laughing children → family fun and relaxation

1 Sound, particularly music, is able to create atmosphere. What type of film would have music of this kind?

	Sound	Type of Film
a)	synthesised music	
b)	orchestral strings predominate	
c)	orchestral drumbeats predominate	
d)	folk music	

2 What instruments would create atmosphere for a programme based in the following countries? Name an instrument from each country.

a) India: ....

b) Pacific Islands: ....

c) Africa: ....

B Myriad Moods

1 Voice tone conveys mood. Write sentences used by characters from your text that were said in these tones of voice:

a) Formal: ....

b) Questioning: ....

c) Concerned: ....

d) Accusing: ....

e) Menacing: ....

f) Reflective: ....

g) Dreamy: ....

C Creating the Mood

1 Choose a moment from the text being studied where mood or atmosphere is significant and explain why it is important.

[✓ Checkpoint in answers] ....

Achievement Standard 1.5 - Test

Write about one visual or oral text you have studied in class.

Choose one question. Write about 200 words. Support your points with specific details from the text.

	1	Describe the key idea dealt with in the text. Why is this key idea important?
OR	2	Describe the opening sequence that creates the setting. Why is it important?
OR	3	Describe an important character and explain why he/she is important.
OR	4	Describe a critical moment in the text. Explain why this moment is critical.
OR	5	Choose several production features that support the text well and show how they are important. You could choose music, sound track, special effects, lighting, colour, graphics, camera work, make-up.

I have selected question number ....

You may need to continue on refill.

90 Meaning

The meaning of a text is gained by an appreciation of the techniques used to create that meaning. Unfamiliar texts may include creative writing, poetry, posters or the text of a speech.

A Thinking Analytically

By asking questions we can test the ability of the reader to understand the meaning of a passage.

Example:

Explain in your own words what the expression 'cool head' means.

OR Why do you think the boy's name is not mentioned?

1 Explain the meaning of the underlined words in each sentence.

a) *Am I losing my inner perception of my cultural identity?*

....

....

....

....

b) *I think about things beyond the Samoan 'mode' of house chores, dinner and prayers set out for Samoans my age.*

....

....

....

....

B We Are Aotearoa

1 Explain how the design in the centre of the advertisement supports the slogan.

....

....

....

....

....

....

....

....

....

....

....

....

....

....

....

C 'The Builders'

1 Read this poem by Sara Henderson Hay carefully, then answer the questions that follow.

The Builders

I told them a thousand times if I told them once:
Stop fooling around, I said, with straw and sticks;
They won't hold up; you're taking an awful chance.
Brick is the stuff to build with, solid bricks.
You want to be impractical, go ahead.
But just remember, I told them; wait and see.
You're making a big mistake. Alright, I said,
But when the wolf comes, don't come running to me.

The funny thing is, they didn't. There they sat,
One in his crummy yellow shack, and one
Under his roof of twigs, and the wolf ate
Them hair and hide. Well, what is done is done.
But I'd been willing to help them along, all along,
If only they'd once admitted they were wrong.

Sara Henderson Hay

a) Who is the narrator of this poem?

....

b) What is the tone of the poem?

....

c) What clues are given that lead you to this conclusion regarding the tone.

....

....

d) Explain why the narrator repeats the word 'brick' in Line 4.

....

....

e) What is the crummy yellow shack?

....

Style is the way an author chooses to write. A writer may wish to persuade, inform, describe, amuse, or question a situation.
In general terms writing styles may be: formal, humorous, emotional, persuasive, ironic, dramatic, colloquial, questioning

A Writer's Words

1 Write one sentence that illustrates each style of writing.

a) Formal Writing ....

b) Persuasive Writing ....

c) Colloquial Writing ....

d) Emotional Writing ....

e) Dramatic Writing ....

B Continuing in Style

1 Choose one of the styles of writing listed in the hint line above. Write a paragraph of your own in that style of writing.

....

D Marvellous Montage

1 From any source available: newspapers, magazines, instructions, poetry, song lyrics, letters (formal and informal) etc. make a collection of various styles of writing, create a montage and label each writing style with its source.

92 Types of Sentences

A sentence may be minor, simple, compound or complex as well as being a statement, question, exclamation or command.

A Circles and Lines

A sentence has two parts:

1 The person or thing being written about. (subject)

2 What that person or thing does. (predicate)

Tom (subject) | stepped on his skateboard (predicate)

1 Circle the subject and underline the predicate of this sentence.

Laura swung onto her horse.

2 Underline the main clauses that make this a compound sentence.

Laura swung onto her horse and she settled into the saddle.

3 Circle the subordinate clause in this complex sentence.

Laura swung onto her horse when she had to enter the show ring.

4 Explain why this is a minor sentence: "Sure thing."

....

....

....

B Strictly Structural

1 Write a sentence that illustrates clearly your understanding of these types of sentence structure.

Statement ....

....

Question ....

....

Exclamation ....

....

Command ....

....

2 Explain what part each of the following plays in the structure of a sentence.

Phrase ....

....

Clause ....

....

C Flowers and Sympathy

1 Read this conversation between two friends then answer the questions below.

"Have you seen Julie?"
"No, not today."
"I wish she'd hurry up and come."
"I think she was sick last night so maybe she's still unwell."
"Really? I didn't know!"
"Perhaps I'll buy some flowers and a card and go and see her."
"Sounds cool."

GET WELL

From this conversation write one example of each of the following:

a) Simple Sentence: ....

b) Compound Sentence: ....

c) Complex Sentence: ....

d) Question: ....

e) Exclamation: ....

f) Phrase: ....

Your vocabulary is the words you know. To continue to increase your vocabulary will give fluency and precision to your work.

A Get It Right!

1 What words should have been used instead of the underlined word?

a) Her aunt is a superfluous and spiteful woman.

....

b) Sarah wont to the optimist to have her eyes tested.

....

c) The obsolescent was expert at putting off his chores.

....

d) It is important to understand the prototype of other cultures.

....

e) The passenger arrived at the terminate to check-in her luggage.

....

f) Nicola had an affection in her right eye.

....

g) The business organisation was corroded.

....

h) The oldest building in town was declared a hysterical site.

....

i) With parental support he decided to go on to territory study.

....

j) The iron man competition is for the ulterior athlete.

....

B Two By Two

1 Beside each word write two synonyms.

a) cautious ....

b) dismiss ....

c) energetic ....

d) forgive ....

2 Beside each word write two antonyms.

a) praise ....

b) rude ....

c) reassure ....

d) encourage ....

3 Add a prefix to each of the following to alter its meaning.

a) appear ....

b) important ....

c) practical ....

d) conduct ....

e) correct ....

4 Add a suffix to each of the following to alter its meaning.

a) prince ....

b) magic ....

c) cigar ....

d) meaning ....

e) child ....

C Horrible Homonyms

1 For each word give two different meanings.

a) brood ❑ ....

❑ ....

b) account ❑ ....

❑ ....

c) casual ❑ ....

❑ ....

94 Parts of Speech

All words can be sorted into groups according to what they do in a sentence. All words that name things are in one group; all words that describe things are in another, and so on. The name of the group that a word belongs to is called its Part of Speech.

Example:	Red	helicopters	flew	swiftly	by	them
	↓	↓	↓	↓	↓	↓
	adjective	noun	verb	adverb	preposition	pronoun

A Parts and Placement

1 From this sentence place each word in the appropriate place in the chart below.

'Samuel Marsden quickly established a mission in the beautiful Bay of Islands where he conducted church services for early settlers.'

a)	proper noun	
b)	noun	
c)	pronoun	
d)	adjective	
e)	verb	
f)	preposition	
g)	adverb	

B Covering All Parts

1 State what part of speech the underlined word represents.

a) A small shoot appeared at the base of the plant.

....

b) I will shoot that possum if I get near it.

....

c) Slowly he climbed to the top of the tree.

....

d) Adam ran until he was exhausted.

....

e) The terrified rabbit leaped for its burrow.

....

f) The kiwi bird is a symbol of New Zealand.

....

g) The poplar trees grew beside the lake.

....

C Playing a Part

Some words may have more than one meaning and so may have more than one part of speech.

Example: The word : *line* 1] A white line was drawn on the road. (noun) 2] The children were asked to line up. (verb)

1 At the end of each sentence state the part of speech that the word plays.

a) That kid is a bit of a worry.	
b) I watched the dog worry the bone.	
c) Business was slow on Mondays.	
d) The vehicle began to slow down at the corner.	
e) Her mother put the key in the lock.	
f) He was a key figure at the meeting.	
g) The horse's hind quarters were injured.	
h) The hind quickly ran into the forest.	

Language features are the ways words are used to achieve a desired effect.

A Bring It On

Every generation uses words that have become features of the language they speak.

Example:	Slang :	Teenagers :	guys,	it sux
		Adults :	super,	smashing
		Elderly :	fed up,	crikey

1 Write two examples for each of the following language features. Include a definition to explain the particular language feature.

a) Slang

Definition: ....

....

Examples: ....

....

b) Colloquialism

Definition: ....

....

Examples: ....

....

c) Jargon

Definition: ....

....

Examples: ....

....

B Playing with Emotions

1 Circle the word that has a negative connotation in each of the following pairs of words.

a)	skinny	slim
b)	girl	sheila
c)	crusty	old
d)	ankle-biter	child
e)	police	fuzz
f)	elderly	wrinklies
g)	extravagant	generous
h)	scruffy	worn
i)	pushed	barged
j)	inexpensive	cheap

2 Choose one of the pairs of words listed in the exercise above and explain the emotional effect that is created by each word.

....

....

....

....

....

....

C Playing with Emotions

1 Read this extract on bullying. Answer the questions that follow by circling the appropriate answer.

'One in eight children aged 9-12 years is being subjected to physical violence at school. The findings come from a survey conducted during the year, in which questionnaires were filled out by 1946 students. Overall 69 percent of students said they were victims of violence and verbal abuse. Nearly half of those surveyed (49 per cent) admitted being violent toward other students and boys were a lot more likely to be perpetrators than girls.

a) What is the general tone of the article?

sarcastic   objective   informal

b) From what point of view is the article written?

1st person (I)   2nd person (you)   3rd person (they)

c) What is the purpose of writing?

to amuse   influence   inform   persuade

d) Who is the target audience?

pre-teens   teenagers   adults

e) To what genre does this article belong?

magazine   novel   short story   newspaper

96 Adjectives

The adjective is a part of speech that describes or gives additional information about a noun and may be placed before or after a noun. Sometimes they are called modifiers because they modify the noun. Adjectives give depth to writing by helping the reader to visualise the image more clearly.

A First and Last

Adjectives may come before or after a noun.

Examples: Before - *The crimson pohutukawa.*
After - *The pohutukawa flower is crimson.*

1 Write phrases where the adjective comes before the noun. Underline the adjective e.g. The valuable ring

a) ....

b) ....

c) ....

d) ....

e) ....

f) ....

2 Write examples where the adjective is after the noun. Underline the adjective e.g. The boy was tired.

a) ....

b) ....

c) ....

d) ....

e) ....

f) ....

3 Replace the underlined adjectives by others that mean the opposite.

a) The stout lady wore a light cardigan.

....

b) Sarah was tall with short curly hair.

....

c) The old watch was slow.

....

d) The apple was large and sweet.

....

e) Cook Strait is often calm and pleasant.

....

B Changing Parts

Adjectives can be formed from other parts of speech.

1 Form an adjective from each noun.

Noun	Adjective
fame	....
comfort	....
sympathy	....
courtesy	....
argument	....
spectacle	....
microscope	....
danger	....
experiment	....
asthma	....

C Melissa Edwards

1 Underline the adjectives in this poem, written by a student, but based on an Iain Sharpe poem.

Melissa Edwards

Melissa Edwards is a split end
Divided into two parts.

Melissa Edwards is a many-layered parcel
Years of unwrapping still don't reveal her.

Melissa Edwards is a golden honeybee
Who gives a sharp sting to unkindness.

Melissa Edwards is a spotted fawn
Shy and wary, gentle with others.

Melissa Edwards is fourteen letters
Wrung from the Roman alphabet.

Wherever I go
Melissa Edwards is there.
Windows, mirrors,
She silently follows me.

Verbs - Tenses

Verbs are actions taken by someone or something. They say what we do, e.g. run, hop, eat, talk, write, speak. They show the past, present and future tense. The past tense tells about actions that have already happened. The present tense tells of actions that are happening now. The future tense refers to actions that will happen.

A Do or Say

1 Place each of these verbs into the correct column in the chart.

munched	shattered
explained	sprawled
pounded	stuttered
applauded	whimpered
sneered	mumbled

Verbs for Actions	Verbs for Speaking
....	....
....	....
....	....
....	....
....	....

B How Is It Done?

1 Add two adverbs to show how each of these actions could be done. Use different adverbs for each. One is done for you.

	Verbs	Adverbs
a)	ate	*hungrily, greedily*
b)	bounced	....
c)	chewed	....
d)	climbed	....
e)	grasped	....
f)	lifted	....
g)	moved	....
h)	shouted	....

C Verbs Only

1 Circle the verbs in these proverbs.

a) A drowning man clutches at straws.

b) A rolling stone gathers no moss.

c) Birds of a feather flock together.

d) Cut your coat according to your cloth.

e) Look before you leap.

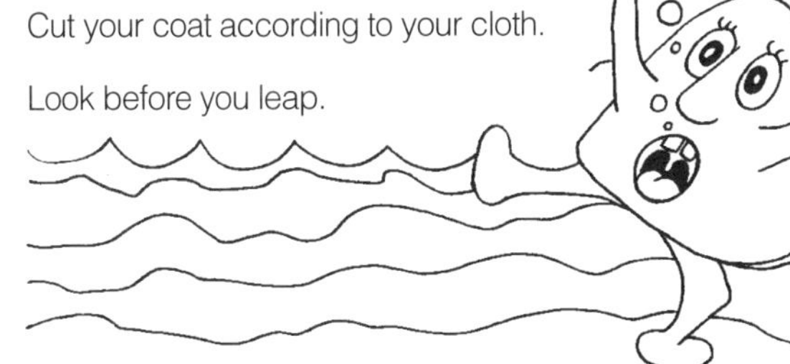

D Know Your Tenses

In a piece of writing, the tenses must not be confused.

1 Complete this chart by filling in the gaps.

Past Tense	Present Tense	Future Tense
a)	a) *I am biting.*	a) ....
b) *I have driven.*	b)	b) ....
c)	c)	c) *I will sing.*
d)	d) *I know.*	d) ....
e)	e) *I am crying.*	e) ....

Adverbs

An adverb tells how, when, where or why something happens. It is a part of speech that describes or qualifies a verb or adjective. When the work of an adverb is done by a group of words, the group is called an adverbial phrase. Most adverbs end in -ly. They help make writing more precise and give further depth to your writing.

A How? When? Where? Why?

An adverb tells more about the meaning of other parts of speech.

Example:

The star shone brightly (how)

The star shone brightly early in the evening (when)

The star shone brightly early in the evening to the south of the mountain (where)

1 List six adverbs or adverbial phrases for each question. One example is given for you to follow in each.

a) *anxiously* .... (How?) ....

b) *occasionally* .... (When?) ....

c) *there* .... (Where?) ....

d) *to get fit* .... (Why?) ....

B Adding to Change

1 Change these adjectives to adverbs with -ly endings.

	adjective	adverb
a)	desperate	....
b)	weary	....
c)	abundant	....
d)	foolish	....
e)	courteous	....
f)	weak	....
g)	audible	....

C Ask Yourself

1 In the box at the end of each sentence write How? When? Where? or Why? to show the kind of explanation given by the adverb or phrase.

	Sentence	
a)	Dinner is on the table.	
b)	We found the bag yesterday.	
c)	The student walked slowly.	
d)	We are late because of the rain.	
e)	He argued fiercely.	
f)	Tomorrow we visit Rotorua.	
g)	I put my book down on the floor.	

D Add Adverbs

1 Complete the following by adding different adverbs.

She sang ....

She slept ....

He painted ....

He looked ....

She smiled ....

She listened ....

He fought ....

He sighed ....

She followed ....

He thought ....

A simile is a phrase which compares two things and uses 'like' or 'as'. Similes help to create mood and atmosphere in writing. Writing that makes use of similes creates images in the mind of the reader.

Example: The wind was bitterly cold.

Simile: The bitterly cold wind cut through him like a knife. or As sharp as a knife, the bitterly cold wind cut through him.

A Smart Similes

1 Complete these sentences by using a simile.

a) The windows of the old house gazed inscrutably like

....

b) He stood on the cliff edge like a ...., eyes seeking a pathway down.

c) The kuia smiled broadly, eyes shining like ....

....

d) The duvet, as .... as a ...., lay on the bed.

B Underline Then Explain

1 Underline the similes in each of these sentences then explain precisely what they mean in this context.

a) His father paced and roared like a lion when confronted with his son's disobedience.

....

....

b) The circling mountains cupped the valley like the hand of a giant.

....

....

c) As quick as a wink the player grasped the ball and threw himself at the try line.

....

....

C The Field

1 Complete this paragraph by adding a simile in each space. Note that the simile must support the descriptive passage before it.

The field stretched flat and square like a .... to the edge of the gully, on the far side of which, eucalyptus trees with torn and shredded trunks lifted white branches .... to the cloud-feathered sky. Dark and sombre like .... pointed pines crouched and menaced intruders from sheltering beneath their grasping boughs along the field's perimeter.

D As Easy as Pie

1 Similes are used every day in conversation and in writing to create images. Complete these well-known similes

a) as blind as ....
b) as busy as ....
c) as cheeky as ....
d) as flat as ....
e) as bright as ....
f) as clear as ....
g) as deaf as ....
h) as brown as ....
i) as quiet as ....
j) as sober as ....
k) as tough as ....
l) as sour as ....
m) as thick as ....
n) as white as ....
o) as bold as ....
p) as hard as ....

100 Metaphors

A metaphor compares two things by saying one thing is something else. It is a direct comparison and does not use 'like' or 'as'. Metaphors create detailed images in the mind of the reader.

Examples: The moon is a ship that sails the sky. A spider is a silk weaver. A fish is a silver bullet of the sea. A cat is king of the house.

A Making Clear

1 What do you think a writer wants to convey to the reader when these metaphors are used?

a) The wind is a knife

....

....

....

b) Her lips are ripe strawberries.

....

....

....

c) The sky is black velvet sequined with silver stars.

....

....

....

B It is a ...

1 Complete the following with imaginative and descriptive metaphors of your own.

a) The windsurfer is ....

....

....

b) A skateboarder is ....

....

....

c) The parapenter is a ....

....

....

d) Pizza is ....

....

....

C What is . . . a Star?

This poem, written by a student, compares a star with a number of things. List these seven comparisons on the right.

What is . . . A Star?

What is . . . A Star?
A star is a fragment of glitter
Young children have placed on black paper.
It is an opening of a tunnel
Far, far away.
It is an arcade of dreams
Where we all go when we sleep.
A star is a precious stone
In the crown of the night.
It is a raindrop
Frozen in the sky.
It is a magical flower
Glowing in a dark field.
A star is a lost fairy
Searching for the moon.

1 What is ..... A Star?

a) ....

b) ....

c) ....

d) ....

e) ....

f) ....

g) ....

2 What other comparisons could be made for a star?

a) ....

b) ....

c) ....

d) ....

Personification

Personification is a figure of speech where things are described as if they were human. Non-living things are referred to as if they have thoughts and feelings.

Examples: The willow tree wept tears of spring rain. The trail of ants marched in file up the pathway. The ditch digger chewed the earth.

A Giving Life

1 What non-living thing could be described as having the following human qualities? Write the name of a non-human thing in the space left in the sentence.

a) The .... scrabbled in the dirt with iron hands.

b) The .... raised its arms to allow the boat to pass underneath.

c) Across the countryside strode giant .... carrying electrical energy.

d) .... danced and leaped along the shell-covered sand.

B Human Qualities

1 Following the examples given in A write four imaginative sentences using personification.

a) ....

....

....

b) ....

....

....

c) ....

....

....

d) ....

....

....

C Be Creative

Personification helps create mood and atmosphere.

1 Create mood and atmosphere by completing these sentences. [✓ Checkpoint in answers]

a) The old pine crouched darkly ....

b) With a snarl the wind ....

c) Shouting and roaring ....

d) Laughing and chattering ....

e) With freezing fingers ....

D Human Habits

1 Choose a subject that lends itself to the use of personification (landforms, the sea, machinery and even computers are some) and write some sentences emphasising the human qualities of that subject.

....

....

....

....

....

....

Alliteration

Alliteration is a sound effect where adjacent or closely connected words begin with the same sound. Using alliteration in writing gives emphasis to the passage by creating an interesting effect.

Examples: 1] The car started with a spit and sputter. 2] Bloody and bowed, the warriors hid in the cave.

A So Simple

1 Add alliterative words to begin each of the following sentences.

a) .... the old car moved slowly up the hill.

b) .... the mud pool made patterns over its surface.

c) ....several seagulls dipped and skimmed over the bay.

d) .... the train pulled the long tail of wagons.

e) .... the waves swept up the storm-ravaged beach.

f) ....the dog looked fearful as his owner approached with a stick in his hand.

B Feeling Free

1 Using the examples you have completed in A as models, write sentences of your own on a variety of subjects.

Allow your imagination to fly! Don't restrict your thinking!

a) ....

....

....

b) ....

....

....

c) ....

....

....

d) ....

....

....

C A Touch Too Much

It is important when using sound devices that they are not overused otherwise the effectiveness is lost.

1 Delete some of the alliteration by drawing a line through those words that overdo the effect required.
Write alliterative sentences of your own in d) and e) taking care not to overdo the effect.

a) With a gasp of fear, Tom crouched behind the tree while the frightening, fearful, fiendish phantom stalked silently by.

b) A short, shrill, shredded shriek cut the air sending the hair standing on the back of Paula's neck.

c) The booming, bumping, boisterous beat of the drums blasted unrestrained through the wide-open wooden-framed windows.

d) ....

....

....

e) ....

....

....

Onomatopoeia is the use of words that imitate or suggest the sound of what they describe. Using onomatopoeia in writing gives vividness by adding sound effects to sentences.

Examples: The seagull screamed as it swooped to gather the food scraps.
The rumble of the train echoed through the valley.
The crack of a whip was a signal to start the cattle drive.

A By Association

1 Write onomatopoeic words for each of the following. Do not repeat any words.

a) water ....splash........ ....roar........
b) guitar ....
c) chains ....
d) baby ....
e) dry leaves ....
f) siren ....
g) boiling kettle ....
h) fire ....
i) clock ....
j) rusty hinges ....

B Wartime

1 Place an interesting onomatopoeic word in the sentence space.

a) The .... of a distant plane disturbed the quiet.
b) A .... of gunfire echoed over the valley.
c) The .... of falling bombs exploding was followed by a brief silence.
d) A long drawn-out .... of terror reverberated over the rooftops.
e) Broken bricks .... as rescuers scrambled towards the source of the painfilled voice.

2 Circle the ten words that are onomatopoeic.

clatter	ripple	pluck	hiss
rain	wash	tinkle	call
lap	crack	burn	shriek
break	boast	growl	echo
gush	shout	plunge	drive

C Sound Wordsearch

1 In the wordfinder you will find the onomatopoeic word that best describes the sound made by each of the following. Circle each one as you find it then place it in the space provided.

a) The .... of a whip.
b) The .... of a train.
c) The .... of escaping air.
d) The .... of a frog.
e) The .... of a hurt dog.
f) The .... of a bullet.
g) The .... of machinery.
h) The .... of waves.
i) The .... of flies.
j) The .... of a wolf.

S	Z	L	C	R	A	C	K
U	W	Z	M	U	H	R	R
P	H	S	U	M	P	O	I
H	I	S	S	B	P	A	T
C	N	L	I	L	A	K	C
K	E	C	Y	E	L	P	O
U	L	W	O	H	S	G	H

The leftover letters make up a series of four sound words. List them here:

....
....

Figures of Speech

Figures of speech give colour to writing through images created in the mind, the sound the words make or the message received by the way words are used or the tone in which they are said.

A Creating Images

1 For each figure of speech listed, write a definition followed by an example or two to show your understanding.

Figure of Speech	Definition	Examples of Use
simile		
metaphor		
personification		

2 Creating Sounds

Figure of Speech	Definition	Examples of Use
alliteration		
assonance		
onomatopoeia		
rhyme		

3 Word Use and Tone

Figure of Speech	Definition	Examples of Use
pun		
hyperbole		
rhetorical question		
imperative		

Hyphenation

A hyphen is used when a compound word is formed from two words. A hyphen is also used to divide a word when it does not fit on a line. It can only be used between syllables to divide a word into two parts of at least two letters on each line. A hyphen is also used to divide compound words when they do not fit a line. The hyphen goes between the two words.

Examples: two-step method sister-in-law
Examples: collect = col-lect bellow = bel-low
Example: fingerprint = finger-print If a double consonant is in the middle of a word, the word is usually divided there.

A Divide

1 Place hyphens in the appropriate places to divide these words.

a) i n t o
b) w i t h o u t
c) w h i t e b o a r d
d) a n g r y
e) c r y s t a l
f) c r u n c h y
g) f r o s t b i t e
h) r e g r e t f u l
i) l e v e r a g e
j) m i s t a k e n

2 What are each of the following? Write a brief definition.

a) brain-teaser ....
b) dust-up ....
c) flip-flop ....
d) get-together ....
e) high-flyer ....

B Two Behave as One

1 Join the first column with the second by drawing an arrow between the words that are hyphenated and behave as one word.

a)	narrow-	old
b)	off-	off
c)	part-	handed
d)	right-	colour
e)	take-	minded
f)	second-	time
g)	age-	generation

2 Add an ending of your own to create compound words.

a) apple..........
b) blind..........
c) class..........
d) day..........
e) ear..........
f) fool..........
g) gate..........
h) heart..........
i) ink..........
j) jaw..........

C Relations

1 Write the plural to each of the following hyphenated words.

mother-in-law ....
father-in-law ....
sister-in-law ....
brother-in-law ....
son-in-law ....
daughter-in-law ....

D Really Brief

1 Give a brief meaning to each of the following hyphenated words.

a)	fire-watcher	
b)	dog-tired	
c)	hold-up	

106 Punctuation

Punctuation is the name given to the marks used in writing to separate sentences and their elements, and to clarify meaning.

A All You Need

1 For each punctuation mark write a definition of its use and then complete the chart by writing an example of its use. Use books, newspapers and magazines to help you find examples.

Punctuation Mark	Definition	Examples of Use
full stop .		
comma ,		
apostrophe 's isn't		
inverted commas “ ” ‘ ’		
question mark ?		
exclamation mark !		
colon :		
semicolon ;		
dash —		
hyphen -		
brackets ( )		
ellipsis . . .		

Question One : Reading Written Texts

Text A (Written Text). After reading this, answer questions 1-5.

I heard a heavy step approaching behind the great door and saw through the chinks the gleam of a coming light. Then there was the sound of rattling chains and the clanking of massive bolts drawn back . . . and the huge door swung open.

Within stood a tall old man, clean-shaven save for a long white moustache and clad in black from head to foot without a single speck of colour on him anywhere. His face was strong - very strong - with a high bridge to the aquiline nose and peculiar arched nostrils; with lofty domed forehead and hair growing scantily round the temples but profusely elsewhere. His eyebrows were massive, almost meeting over the nose. The mouth, as far as I could see it under the heavy moustache, was fixed rather cruel-looking with peculiar sharp white teeth; these protruded over the lips whose remarkable ruddiness showed astonishing vitality for a man of his years.

from 'Dracula' by Bram Stoker

1 From anywhere in the passage write down one word that shows this passage is written in the first person. ....

2 Why have dashes been used in Line 4? ....

3 Circle the synonym for each word.

aquiline	hooked	prominent	distinctive
profusely	extravagantly	lavishly	plentifully
protruded	extended	bulged	elongated

4 What is meant by the *'gleam of a coming light'*?

....

....

....

5 In your own words explain how Bram Stoker creates tension in the first paragraph.

....

....

....

....

....

....

....

....

....

....

....

....

....

Achievement Standard 1.6 - Test 2

Question One : Reading Written Texts

Text B (Written Text). After reading this, answer questions 1-4.

Pukeko

Strutting these swamps before the settlers came
He ruled here once. Now his lush land
Fattens the farmer's purse he walks in fear,
Splaying his big feet in ungainly flight.
Poor Porphyrio, tolerated clown;
Common, they called him, loud - all flashy blue
And flaunting scarlet, Cousin Notornis, now,
He's somebody; this one's a common pest.

Dusk over the plains: and lord of the swamp once more
Stalking from secret raupo haunts inviolate
He takes his tithes with condescending strut
While the sad bittern's booming in the marsh
That morning comes too soon, too soon, he's high above,
His harsh triumphant cry strung on the wind.

Barbara Free

1 What is the pukeko (line 5) compared to?

2 What is the meaning of the word 'condescending' (line 11)?

3 Why do you think the pukeko is described as *'common'* and *'loud'* (line 6)?

4 What does the poet, Barbara Free, think of the pukeko in relation to the notornis?

Question Two : Reading Visual Texts

Text C (Visual Text). After reading this, answer questions 1-4.

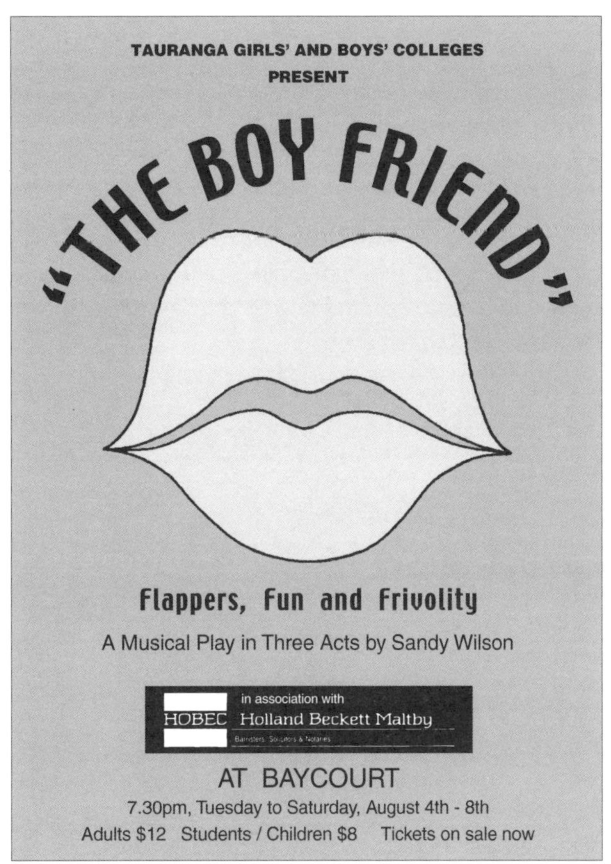

1 If you were asked to choose a background colour for the poster that would contrast strongly with bright red lips, what colour would you choose and why? ....

....

....

2 How does the symbolism of the lips support the title? ....

....

....

....

3 What indicates that this production was sponsored? ....

....

4 Name a language feature that has been used. ....

Write down the phrase that contains this language feature. ....

....

Achievement Standard 1.6 - Test 4

Question Three : Reading Oral Texts

Text D (Oral Text). After reading this, answer questions 1-4.

Short? Short? Have you ever given any thought to what it is like to be short? Most people never do. Most people have no idea what it is like to be shorter than the average. It's a small matter to most.

Imagine yourself at a sports match where there is no grandstand and you're stuck behind rows of sporty types that resemble a pine forest. The only view you get is a brief glimpse at waist level - it's like glimpsing a view through vertical venetian blinds and if you try the alternative of bouncing up and down as if on an invisible trampoline all you get is pitying grins. It's no use getting down on hands and knees, you're likely to get trampled underfoot!

Growing up shorter than normal has other drawbacks too. A pat on the head accompanied by " Good things come in small parcels" can be astonishingly aggravating after the thousandth time. It is a wonder short people don't bite the ankles of those who make such condescending remarks.

Being short can have a positive side as well. You can buy clothes from the children's department, pay half price at movies and get other people to hang out the washing!

Do I want to be short? Not likely!

1 Identify an example where the speaker uses a list in the speech.

....

....

2 Identify the language technique used in *'It's a small matter to most.'* (line 2). ....

3 What is the purpose of this speech? ....

....

4 How does the speaker involve the audience? ....

....

....

5 Choose a language technique such as rhetorical question, contrast, imagery, alliteration or repetition that the speaker has used and explain why it has been used.

....

....

....

....

....

....

....

....

....

Topic Choice

You should allow the type of occasion and the age group of your audience to influence your topic choice and the way you deliver the speech.

A Type Choices

1 Write descriptions that explain these different kinds of speech.

a)	Prepared Speech
b)	Impromptu Speech
c)	Memorised Speech
d)	Scripted Speech
e)	Whaikorero

B Broadly Speaking

1 Some topics may be too broad for a speech topic and need to be narrowed down. Narrow each of these broad topics to make them suitable for a speech.

a)	'New Zealand's Natural Features.'
b)	'Global Warming and its Consequences.'
c)	'Fashion through the Ages.'
d)	'Famous People.'
e)	'Music from around the World.'
f)	'Sea Creatures.'
g)	'Exploration.'

C Keep This in Mind

1 What should the speaker keep in mind when delivering a speech to each of these audiences? Write three or four points.

a)	Pre-Teens	
b)	Teenagers	
c)	Adults	
d)	Senior Citizens	
e)	Maori Audience	

112 Purpose

The purpose of a formal speech may be to entertain, influence, persuade, inform or explain as well as welcome and thank others for a particular reason. There is always an audience involved. [N.B. Many ideas in this section are also tested in AS1.6 at the end of the year.]

A Suitable Selection

1 Write the name of a speech topic that would be suitable for each of the following purposes.

a)

Entertainment : light-hearted, uses humour

b)

Special Occasions : farewells, funerals, reunions

c)

Information : presents facts, uses visual aids

d)

Persuasion : points of view, emotive language

B Top Topics

1 Write the names of a selection of topics suitable for a Year 11 student audience where the purpose of the speech is to persuade. [✓ Checkpoint in answers]

a) ....

....

b) ....

....

c) ....

....

d) ....

....

e) ....

....

2 Of these topics which one do you prefer to follow up?

....

....

C Mind Mapping

1 Write the name of a speech topic that interests you in the oval in the middle. Then, without a pause, write associated ideas, facts and phrases (try for 20-25) around the central topic. Highlight those you feel could be key words for your speech and may be useful for further research.

Theme 113

The theme of a speech is the subject or topic on which a person speaks and the message the speaker conveys to the audience about that topic.

A Thinking Themes

1 What message would you want an audience to hear from you on each of the following topics?

School Uniforms
Immigration
G.E. Food
Teens - The Forgotten Section of Society
Couch Potatoes vs Fitness Freaks

B Developing Themes

1 Using two of the topics mentioned in A write two or three main points for each that could be developed to reinforce the theme of the speech.

a) Topic : ....

Theme : ....

Main points :

1 ....

2 ....

3 ....

b) Topic : ....

Theme : ....

Main points :

1 ....

2 ....

3 ....

C Expanding a Theme

1 Using a topic you have chosen, carefully amplify the theme by writing expanded notes for the two or three main points.

Your Topic : .... [✓ Checkpoint in answers]

Point No. 1 ❑ ....

....

....

Point No. 2 ❑ ....

....

....

Point No. 3 ❑ ....

....

....

114 Researching

To gather information for a speech it is wise to use a wide variety of resources rather than just one source.

A Looking and Searching

1 Using the headings given as guidelines, list sources you could use to gather material from for your speech.

School Sources: ....

....

Community Sources: ....

....

Library Sources: ....

....

Print Sources: ....

....

Electronic Sources: ....

....

B Foundations First

1 Write three statements that will form the basis of your speech. Write a reason or example that will support each statement.

Statement 1 ....

....

....

....

....

Statement 2 ....

....

....

....

....

Statement 3 ....

....

....

....

....

C Investigating Material

1 There are ten resource ideas in the wordsearch. Only the first two letters of each word and the number of letters in brackets are given as clues. Circle the word found then complete the word listed. (Look in every direction.) The letters left over make up a hidden message.

a) .... **st** .... (10)

b) .... **qu** .... (10)

c) .... **su** .... (7)

d) .... **in** .... (10)

e) .... **en** .... (12)

f) .... **li** .... (7)

g) .... **vi** .... (5)

h) .... **ne** .... (10)

i) .... **CD** .... (5)

j) .... **ex** .... (7)

E	N	C	Y	C	L	O	P	E	D	I	A
S	E	T	H	E	B	A	S	I	S	N	O
N	W	F	A	O	E	X	P	E	R	T	S
O	S	N	I	E	N	T	S	E	R	E	E
I	P	S	T	D	I	Y	N	C	G	R	S
T	A	P	E	I	E	E	C	D	H	V	I
A	P	S	S	V	Y	R	A	R	B	I	L
T	E	K	R	I	L	F	U	O	L	E	R
O	R	U	E	S	E	A	R	M	C	W	H
U	S	T	A	T	I	S	T	I	C	S	A
Q	N	D	S	E	L	E	C	T	I	O	N

2 The message is : ....

Information that has been gathered for a speech should be arranged in hearer-friendly order.

A Storing Ideas

1 The scrambled letters indicate some ways research material for speeches may be organised. Unscramble them.

a) d a c r s ....

b) l i e s f ....

c) t a d a s s e a b ....

d) i n i n e x d g ....

2 Explain briefly why it is important to research speech material.

....

B Bringing Order

1 Write a constructive hint about organising information using either of these phrases :
- ❏ order of importance
- ❏ chronological order

....

C Time Ticks Away

1 Is the material that you have gathered sufficient to allow you to speak for the time required?
Use this diagram to help you plan what you will say in each of the three minutes allowed for your speech.

First Minute 01

Second Minute 02

Third Minute 03

The Approach

The approach taken in a speech is how the subject is dealt with by the speaker. Usually speeches are either humorous or serious. A speaker must feel comfortable with the approach they decide to take. It is often harder to successfully deliver a humorous speech.

A Laugh or Frown

1 For each speech topic given, briefly indicate how it could be approached in either a serious or humorous fashion.

a) 'Tomatoes'

Serious : ....

....

....

Humorous : ....

....

....

b) 'Examinations - Internal or External?'

Serious : ....

....

....

Humorous : ....

....

....

B Consider and Reflect

1a) Consider the speech you will have to make. Circle the features you think you might use to add impact.

figures of speech
allusions
colloquialisms
irony
imagery
quotations
humour
anecdotes
poetry
repetition

b) Is your preference for speech making serious or humorous?

....

C Moments of Laughter

1 Humour may be introduced in your speech by using one of the following: joke, poem, anecdote, drama, props, others.

a) Where could you use humour in your speech? ....

....

....

....

b) What form (as indicated above) would that humour take? ....

....

....

....

c) What is the purpose of the humour used in your speech? ....

....

....

....

Introduction

A formal speech begins with an introduction of the speech topic that makes an impact on the audience. The audience salutations may go before or after these opening statements.

A Ladies and Gentlemen

1 Give a short explanation of where these opening remarks could be said.

a) 'Members of the staff and students . . .'

....

b) 'Ladies and gentlemen, may I, as chairman, introduce the local Member of Parliament to you . . .'

....

c) 'Kia ora katoa . . .'

....

d) 'Adjudicators, teachers and fellow students . . .'

....

2 Besides the greeting it is important that the audience is made aware of something before the end of the introduction.

What is this? ....

....

B Introductory Remarks

1 Use the listed words to fill in the spaces in each sentence.

viewpoint	points	attention
entertaining	audience	topic
	introductory	

a) Greet the ....

b) Let them know in one sentence what the .... is.

c) How will you get their .... ?

d) Your personal .... is stated in the last sentence of the .... paragraph.

e) Main .... should be included as well.

f) Have an .... opening to gain the audience's attention.

C Who's Listening to You?

1 Write an interesting opening sentence greeting these audiences.

Audience	Opening Sentence
Wedding Guests	
Farmers	
Year 9 Students	
Maori Students	
Foreign Students	
Over 60's	

Body

The body of a speech is the place where the detailed information is delivered to the audience. It informs and explains.

A Body Parts

1 Use these words to fill the spaces in the sentences.

repeat	climax	edit
argument	points	time
	ideas	

a) The body is the main part of the speech where the .... or information is presented.

b) Make four or five .... which will be presented as the basis of your speech.

c) Do not .... any ideas you have already presented.

d) Ideas should lead up to the .... of your speech.

e) .... any weak ideas, or those that don't fit what you wish to say.

f) .... should move smoothly from point to point.

g) Keep to the required ....

B Matching Up

1 Match up the first half of each hint with the correct second half by drawing an arrow between the two.

a) Make brief notes	into separate sections
b) Group ideas	judiciously
c) Strong ideas	on all ideas
d) Edit ideas	that don't fit
e) Make points	are best
f) Get rid of ideas	in the best possible way
g) Say those ideas	clearly

C Considering Ideas

1 Jot down the ideas and techniques you will use when writing the body of your speech. Use the diagram to guide you.

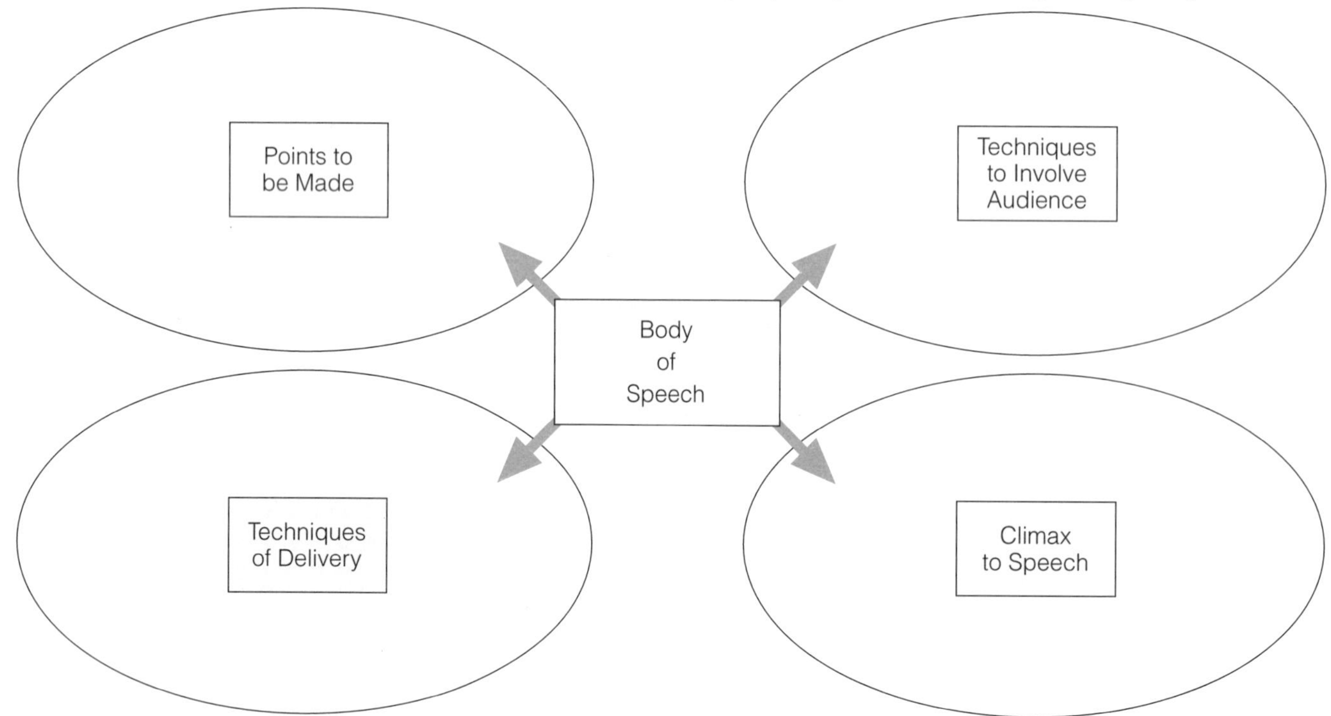

The conclusion is the final section of a speech and sums up the key points. It should leave a good impression with the audience.

A Winding it Up

1 Place the most appropriate word you can think of in the spaces in this paragraph about concluding a speech.

The conclusion is the .... of the speech. It .... the main points already made in the body of the speech and should .... up to the strongest point which should be well .... and memorable for the .... The final sentence should be particularly .... and give the audience something to think about or feel .... to do something. If the last few words take the audience back to the ...., this can have a powerful effect.

B Farewell, Goodbye

Sometimes, at the end of a speech it is necessary to farewell the audience in an appropriate manner.

1 Write a general farewell to thank an adult audience for attending a meeting on a cold winter night.

....
....
....
....
....
....
....
....
....

C Being Critical

1 At some time you have listened to speeches in class made by fellow students. Answer each of the following questions.

a) What was the topic of the best speech you have heard in class? ....
....

b) What made this speech memorable for you? ....
....
....

c) Was the content suited to the audience? In what way? ....
....
....

d) In what way did the speaker involve the audience? ....
....
....

e) Did the ideas presented in the speech flow well from one to another? How was this done? ....
....
....

Language Features

Language features may be used to make a speech more effective. Such features as rhetorical questions, repetition, emotive language, alliteration, imperatives, metaphors and colloquial language help to make a speech more personal and interesting to the listener.

A Proudly Kiwi

1 For a speech on 'What makes me proud to be a New Zealander', write an example to illustrate each of the following language features.

a) Rhetorical question :

....

....

b) Repetition :

....

....

c) Emotive language :

....

....

d) Alliteration :

....

....

e) Imperative :

....

....

B Clever Kiwis

1 Label each of the following examples with the language features it illustrates.

a) I want you to think what New Zealand means to you and your family. ....

b) Once, when I was overseas, I heard 'Now is the Hour' sung by a Swiss choir and I almost burst with pride at being a New Zealander. ....

c) In winter a duvet of snow covers the Southern Alps.

....

d) New Zealanders are generally pretty laid back and have a "she'll be right" attitude. ....

e) New Zealand may be a small country but our achievements in many fields have made our historic figures giants among men. ....

C Effectively Written

1 Write a paragraph for your speech that includes some of the language features mentioned in the exercises above.

....

....

....

....

....

....

....

....

....

....

Impact

Impact means a strong effect. A speaker will try to choose a way of saying things so as to influence the way an audience feels.

A Influence with Impact

1 Tick ✓ the sentences that in your opinion have impact.

a) We *must* preserve our culture as it contributes to who we are. ☐

b) Everyone has a culture of which they can be proud. ☐

c) Am I proud of my culture? Of course I am. It is unique. ☐

d) Most of you will have children to whom you will pass aspects of your culture. ☐

e) Your children will have an *absolute* right to their cultural heritage. ☐

f) Culture stems from our past and leads us to our future. ☐

B Listen Up

1 Imperatives (words that give commands) can add impact. Write sentences that command an audience to do something. One is done for you.

a) Think carefully.

b) ....

....

c) ....

....

d) ....

....

e) ....

....

C Make Them Right

1 Name the language technique the speaker is using. What kind of impact is the speaker trying to create?

a) It is up to each of you to preserve the treasures of your proud heritage so your children are anchored by its richness.

The speaker is using ....

....

b) You, and you, and you, must keep in mind that if your generation fails to pass on your knowledge you are depriving future generations of their cultural inheritance.

The speaker is using ....

....

....

c) Has it ever occurred to you that we are guardians of our culture?

The speaker is using ....

....

d) I am proud of my culture. It is my past. It is who I am. It is my future.

The speaker is using ....

....

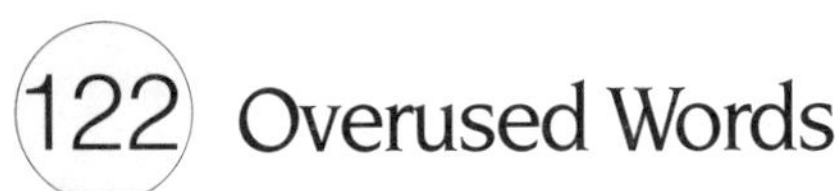

Overused Words

Certain words tend to be used far too much and their impact is lost. It is better to use a more precise alternative to help give quality to your work. Here is an example where there are far too many overused words (italic words).

Example: It is not *nice* to think of our *lovely* shoreline being decimated of *fantastic* seafood by the *horrible* greed and *awful* lack of responsibility shown by some members of our population.

A Dictionary Definitions

1 Use a dictionary, or a thesaurus to find more precise alternatives for each of these overused words.

	Word	Definition
a)	nice	
b)	lovely	
c)	fantastic	
d)	horrible	
e)	awful	

B Five for One

1 List five words that can be used instead of these overused words.

a) beautiful

b) boring

c) excited

d) scared

C Working to Improve

1 Write two sentences from the draft of your speech that need more impact because of poor word choice. Improve the quality of each sentence by using interesting and more precise alternatives.

a) Original Sentence : ....

Improved Sentence : ....

b) Original Sentence : ....

Improved Sentence : ....

Critical Comment 123

Critical comment on a completed speech will give the speaker an opportunity to see if the correct structure and approach have been made.

A Looking Critically

1 Based on the speech you have written, answer each question.

a) What is the purpose of the speech?

....

b) Who is the intended audience?

....

c) What approach have you taken with the topic?

....

d) What language level have you chosen for your speech?

....

e) How does the language level suit the intended audience?

....

B Structurally Sound

1 Look at the structure of the written speech and comment critically on each of the following aspects and how you have handled the requirements of these aspects.

a) The Introduction : ....

b) The Body : [✓ Checkpoint in answers] ....

c) The Conclusion : ....

C Didn't I Do Well

1 What especially pleases you about the speech you have written? Mention language features you have used well, clever anecdotes, quotes and any positive aspects with which you are pleased.

....

Annotating is adding notes to a text or diagram giving explanations or comments.
Once a speech draft has been completed it should be annotated by the writer using both language features and delivery techniques so that it may be analysed critically and improvements made.

A Tricky Terms

1 Use a dictionary to find the correct definition for these terms in relation to texts.

	Word	Definition
a)	exemplar	
b)	extract	
c)	draft	

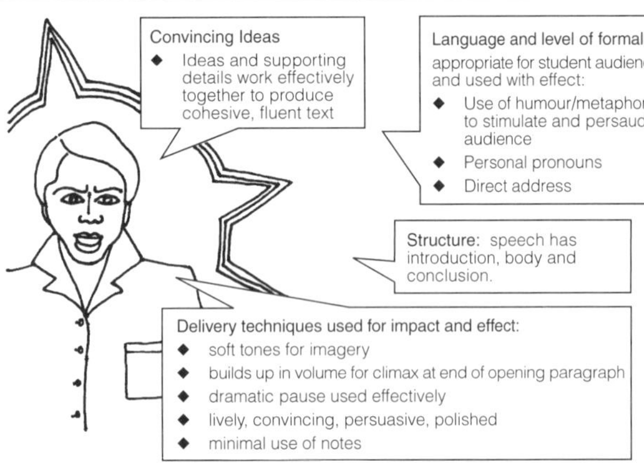

Convincing Ideas
◆ Ideas and supporting details work effectively together to produce cohesive, fluent text
Language and level of formality appropriate for student audience and used with effect:
◆ Use of humour/metaphor to stimulate and persaude audience
◆ Personal pronouns
◆ Direct address
Structure: speech has introduction, body and conclusion.
Delivery techniques used for impact and effect:
◆ soft tones for imagery
◆ builds up in volume for climax at end of opening paragraph
◆ dramatic pause used effectively
◆ lively, convincing, persuasive, polished
◆ minimal use of notes

B Showing the Way

1 Explain why, annotated exemplars are a valuable resource for students writing. (See the illustration for ideas.)

....

....

....

....

....

....

....

....

....

....

....

....

....

....

....

C Speaking with Style

1 List ten features that could be kept in mind when writing the draft of your speech to make it interesting to the audience.

a) ....

b) ....

c) ....

d) ....

e) ....

f) ....

g) ....

h) ....

i) ....

j) ....

Delivering a good speech will require the speaker to use voice techniques and body language

A 'As I Have Said . . .'

1 Unscramble the following to find words that relate to voice techniques.

a) i i t t o o n n n a

b) e e d p s

c) l r c i y a t

d) o u e m l v

e) m s s a e p i h

2 For each of the voice techniques listed above write one sentence that contains advice to a person delivering a speech.

a)

b)

c)

d)

e)

B Stand Tall

1 You are preparing some students for a speech contest. What five tips could you give them to control their nervousness. The word in the brackets will give you a hint.

a) (Stance)

b) (Notes)

c) (Where to look)

d) (Breathing)

e) (Practice)

C What's Wrong

1 Fill in the Delivery Crozzle from the clues given. The word begins where the arrow points.

- one type of speech
- a short stop
- stress on a word
- rate
- loudness
- inflection
- same as solemn
- animated

126 Body Language

Giving a speech is a performance and to support what is said the speaker needs to give a lively delivery.
Body Language is communication made by stance, facial expression and gestures made during the delivery of a speech.

A Define Then Use

1 Write an accurate definition, preferably from a dictionary, for each of these words.

a) stance : ....

....

b) facial expression : ....

....

c) gesture : ....

....

2 Place suitable words in the gaps left in this paragraph.

It is important that the speaker makes .... contact with the .... to include them. Hand .... emphasise important points. The .... of the speaker can convey confidence, pride, purpose and authority. To create a friendly rapport with the audience use .... expressions.

B Body Moves

1 In what situation could a speaker use these movements?

a) A slow shake of the head.

....

....

....

b) Pounding a clenched fist into the palm of the other hand.

....

....

....

c) Nodding confidently.

....

....

....

d) Using a finger to indicate each finger on the other hand.

....

....

....

C Helpful Hidden Words

1 Complete the crossword by using the clues given.

Clue	Letter
a) Your expression should never be this	B
b) A speaker should show this	O
c) Head moves up and down	D
d) Use these to make contact	Y
e) A hand does this to make a fist	L
f) Look long and hard	A
g) A finger does this	N
h) Nodding indicates this	G
i) A movement of the hand	U
j) Side-to-side head movement	A
k) Raised voice indicates this	G
l) How a speaker stands	E

SOAPBOX

A speech presentation can be enhanced by the use of a variety of accessories and props.

A Pleasing Presentation

1 What two or three things could enhance the presentation of a speech on each of the following topics.

a) Maori stick games :

....

....

b) Making pikelets :

....

....

c) School uniforms :

....

....

d) Playing the flute :

....

....

e) Yacht racing :

....

....

B Stand Tall

1 In the area below brainstorm all the visual aids you could use in your speech presentation. Some are given to get you started.

map

video

C Props and Presentation

1 Explain in detail where you intend to use an accessory and/or prop to enhance the presentation of your speech. Explain the effect you wish to achieve with its use. [✓ Checkpoint in answers]

....

....

....

....

....

....

....

....

....

....

Whaikorero

Whaikorero is the making of a speech in Maori.

A Greetings To You

1 Translate these greetings into English.

a) Kia ora ....

b) Haere mai ....

c) Tena koe ....

d) Tena korua ....

e) Tena koutou ....

2 Pukana and Whatero are used in Maori presentations. Write a definition of each term.

a) Pukana ....

....

....

b) Whatero ....

....

....

B On the Marae

1 Place these words into the appropriate place in the paragraph.

waiata	tangata whenua	marae
tokotoko	whaikorero	karanga
	mihimihi	

When visiting a .... it is appropriate to wait outside the marae grounds until a woman of the host tribe calls visitors on with a .... When the visitors have moved onto the marae and silently paid their respects to the ancestors of the .... they are able to sit down. A .... follows when formal speeches are exchanged between men representing the hosts and the guests. .... are made by male elders of the tribe and a ....or oratory stick is used to emphasise what is being said. Each speech is finished with a ....

C Maori Language Week

1 Annotate (add notes to) the following condensed passage. On the left indicate how you would use voice techniques to keep the audience's attention and on the right show where body language features would be used.

The Maori language helps the Maori people to understand their own inheritance as a race. Only the Maori language can adequately express their feelings and emotions as well as their traditions which are interwoven with legend and history. The language, supported by the carvings and weaving which adorn the meeting house, is an intrinsic part of Maori life.

Maori language week is a conscious effort of the two mainstream cultures of this country to understand each other. To understand how people relate to one another and to the world you must understand their language. It can be a means of bringing the two races together to form a better relationship within the community.

The student of another language not only gains an understanding of the people who speak it but they also come to appreciate their own language.

A Talking the Talk

1 Explain what importance each of the following terms has in regard to speech.

a) Purpose of speech :

....

....

....

b) Type of speech :

....

....

....

c) Point of view :

....

....

....

d) Target audience :

....

....

....

B Stand Tall

1 When delivering a speech the voice is used as naturally as possible. Explain why these are important in the control of the voice.

a) Volume of voice :

....

....

....

b) Clarity of voice :

....

....

....

c) Tone of voice :

....

....

....

d) Speed of delivery :

....

....

....

C On with the Performance

Delivering a speech should be a performance and an audience will react to a speaker who shows his / her speech means something.

1 Use the code to find the words that contribute to a speaker's performance.

A	B	C	D	E	F	G	H	I	J	K	L	M	N	O	P	Q	R	S	T	U	V	W	X	Y	Z
2	6	9	13	15	1	19	14	20	10	23	18	24	3	22	25	11	26	17	21	16	4	12	8	7	5

a)

19	15	17	21	16	26	15

b)

15	7	15		9	22	3	21	2	9	21

c)

25	16	23	2	3	2

d)

1	2	9	20	2	18		15	8	25	26	15	17	17	20	22	3

e)

25	2	16	17	15

f)

17	21	2	3	9	15

g)

15	24	25	14	2	17	20	17

h)

12	14	2	21	15	26	22

Assessment Standard 1.7 - Test

Use the following speech, given to new club members of the Little Boots Tramping Club, to make critical comments on either side of the speech. Comment on the following points :

- ❏ structure
- ❏ language features
- ❏ information provided
- ❏ content
- ❏ suitability of greeting
- ❏ conclusion

Also note where aspects of voice delivery, eye contact and body language would be appropriate.

Kia ora and welcome to the Little Boots Tramping Club, an organisation of which I am proud to be a member. My name is Tama Green and I have been a member for five years since I was ten years old. Little Boots is for members ten to seventeen and all the trips we make are supervised by adult members of the Boots Tramping Club, the senior branch of the membership. This year I am the Little Boots Leader, a position you can be elected to by other Little Boots members.

When I first joined I didn't have what I thought was the right gear. You know - tramping boots, wet weather gear, tent, shovel, kitchen sink . . . but I discovered the club introduces its members to their first experiences by having half-day tramps for a few outings to see whether tramping is really what you want to do, and so the equipment needed is fairly basic - good sneakers, shorts, wind-and-waterproof jacket, extra warm clothes and, of course, a day-pack with food - a real essential.

There are plenty of scenic places as well as historic sites in the local area and then, once Little Boots members become more experienced, we visit places further away for a day or weekend which includes an overnight camp. That's really cool.

Everyone learns the ropes gradually. We learn about correct clothing and equipment, how to build shelters and erect tents, the best food to take, how to light fires, cross rivers, read a map and use a compass as well as understand the weather - and that's just the beginning. There are many other aspects of tramping to learn to make sure you and your mates will always be safe.

I would like to thank you all for coming and hope what I have said gives you some idea of what the club offers you. It is always interesting and exciting taking part in the club's activities and you will never regret it if you become a member of this friendly club. See you at the first half-day tramp. Thank you once again. Kia ora.

Colour conveys ideas and creates responses. Colours in a media presentation help give meaning.
[You will find that AS 1.6 will have questions about the content given here.]

Examples : Blues and greens give a cool or cold impression while yellows and reds are warm colours.
Black and white are not considered as colours but are used to contrast, tone and shade. Black is 'sombre or formal', white is 'pure'.

A Symbolic Colours

1 What message can be suggested by the use of these colours? List four to six words representative of that colour.

	Colour	Meaning
a)	Red	***passion***
b)	Yellow	
c)	Green	
d)	Blue	***iciness***
e)	Pink	
f)	White	
g)	Black	***mystery***

B Black and White

1 Contrasting black and white can give different effects.

a) Colour the first Amnesty International symbol black and leave the background white.

b) Colour the background black in the second image and leave the symbol white.

c) What effect does reversing the black and white have on the image?

....

....

....

....

....

....

....

....

....

C Striking Use of Colour

1 Draw a sketch of your own production piece and colour it in. Explain why you chose these colours and what message you wanted to convey with these choices.

....

....

....

....

....

....

....

....

....

Shape and Lines

Shape is the particular form given to something. Shapes used in media may be more effective if they are exaggerated or stylised in some way.
Line is a contour or outline used as a feature of design. Lines are used in design to lead the eye in a particular direction, commonly vertical, horizontal, diagonal or circular.

A Simplify and Stylise

1 Exaggerate or stylise this snail illustration in an interesting way.

B Looking at Lines

1 Draw a simple but effective way of using line to draw the eye in a particular direction. One is completed to help you.
[✓ Checkpoint in answers]

a) vertical

b) horizontal

c) diagonal

d) circular

C Contrasting Ads

1 From newspapers or magazines find two small advertisements that show contrasting ways of using either shape or line.

glue example No. 1 here

glue example No. 2 here

2 Which advertisement do you prefer and why? ....

....

....

Symbolism is the use of things, people and actions to represent ideas.
Different cultures have items or objects that are symbolic of that culture e.g. Maori culture - tiki, moko, kowhaiwhai patterns.

A Symbols of Culture

1 Fill this area with symbols representative of your culture.

My culture is ....

[✓ Checkpoint in answers]

B Make a Montage

1 Cut out or draw examples of symbols to be found in today's world and design a montage using words as well as symbols in this space. Be creative!

C What We Stand For

1 Many countries are recognised by symbols that represent the ideas and qualities of the people. Here is an example. Continue this idea with a country of your choice.

Country :
America

Symbols :
Statue of Liberty, USA Flag

Ideas and Qualities :
freedom, pride, strength

Country :

Symbols :

Ideas and Qualities :

Texture

Texture is the feel, appearance or consistency of a surface or substance. In media, texture is the representation of the tactile quality of a surface.

A Textured Two

1 Find examples of materials found around home to show the contrasting textures indicated. Write their names into the circles.

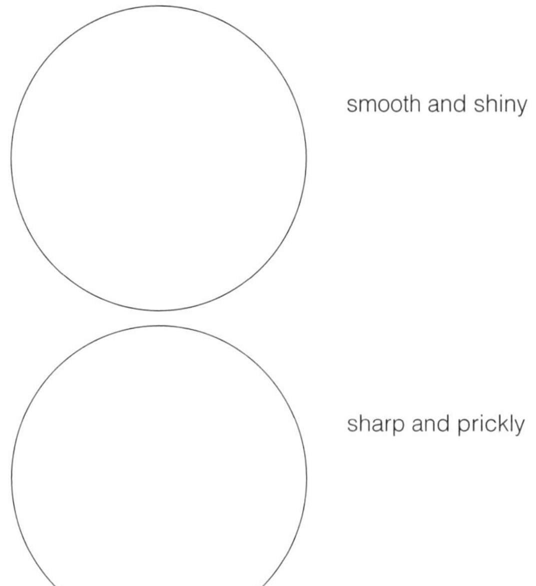

B Simply Surfaces

1 Different textures for a media presentation can be created by using a variety of surfaces. Unscramble these words to find useful surfaces that could be used.

a) p p r a e ....

b) d s a a n p p r e ....

c) r d d b a a o c r ....

d) r c m u l p d e p a e r p ....

e) l o i f ....

f) o u a e d t g r r c r e p a p ....

g) r i c f a b ....

h) p e l l o c h a n e ....

i) d a n s ....

j) d o o w ....

C Tactile Texture

1 Try to give a different feel to each of the following shapes either by drawing different textures or gluing on different surfaces.

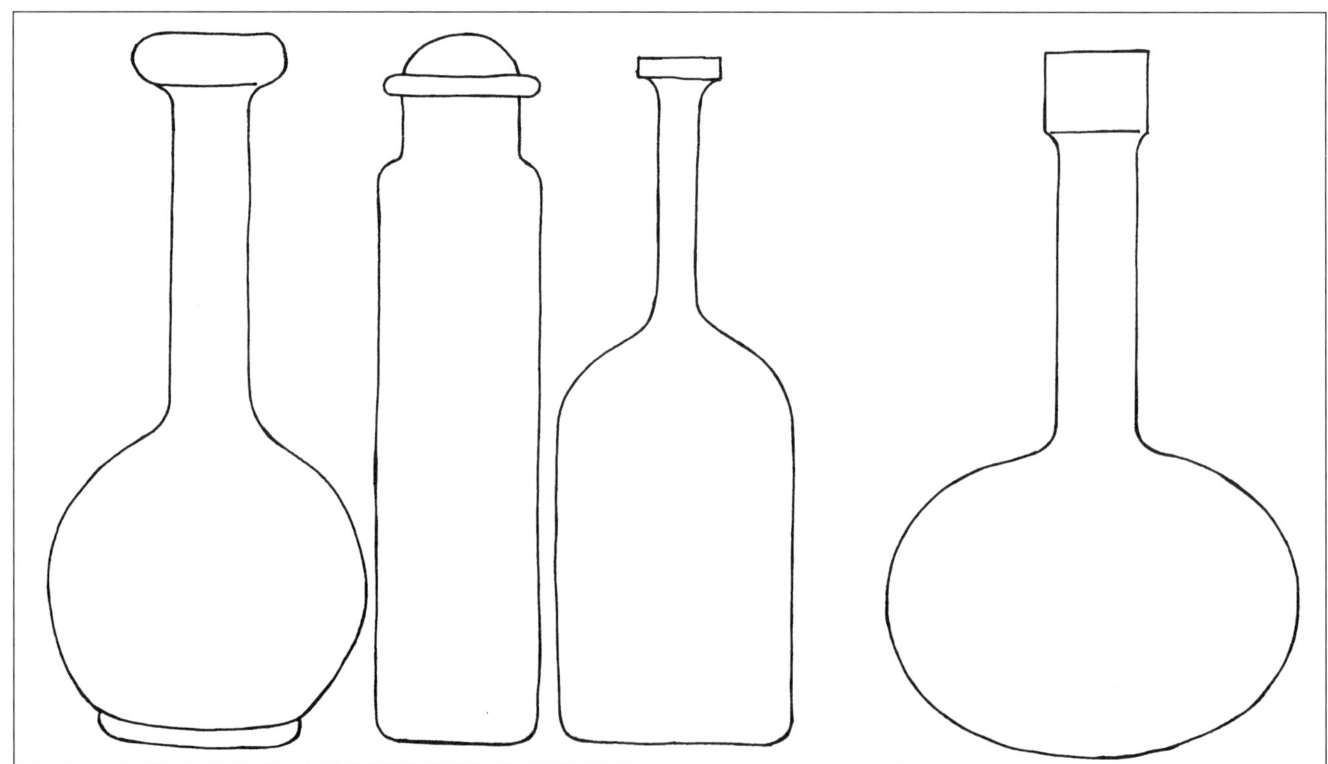

Lettering is the style of typeface in the printed word. The size, shape and appropriateness of the lettering contribute to the impact of the presentation.

A Playing with Names

Words can be written in different ways to give them more impact.

1 Print your first name in this space.

Change the letter shape by using curved lines.

Change the letter shape by using lines with sharp angles.

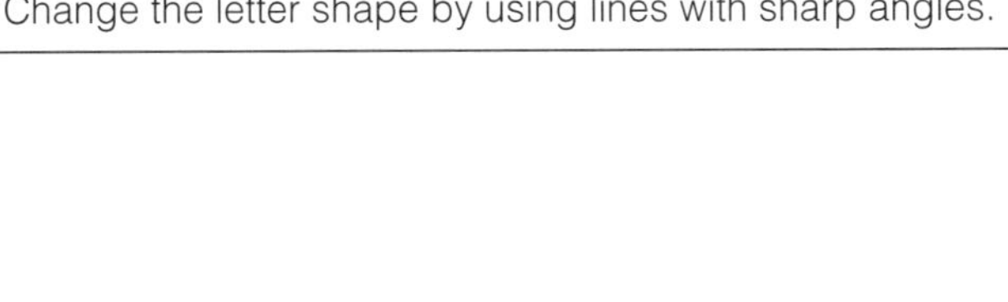

B Bold Fonts

Lettering that is large and bold dominates and should be consistent with the message.

1 Circle the examples that are visually dominant.

a) **BOLD**

b) 

c) **bold**

d) 

e) **bold**

f) **bold**

C Fast Food

1 Select a font and add the words 'fast food' to this poster so that they add to the impact. You may add additional information or work to enhance the poster. [✓ Checkpoint in answers]

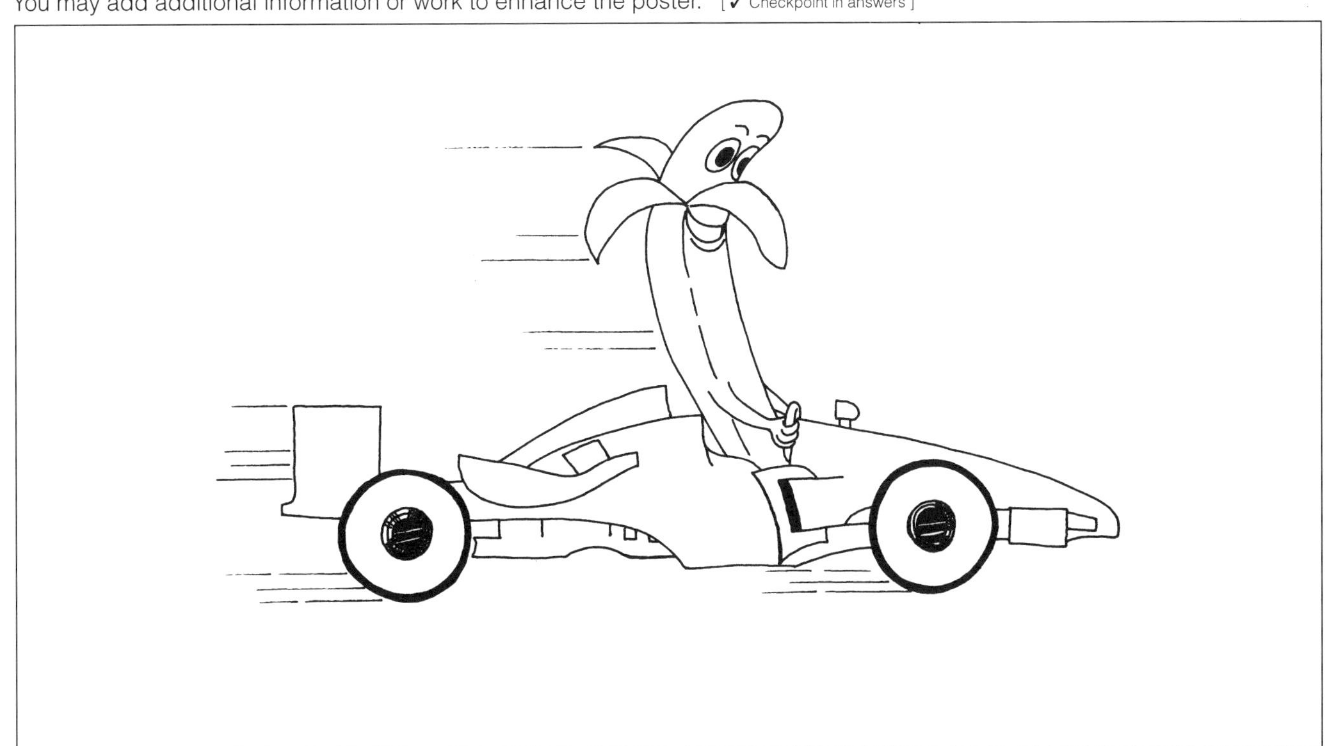

Layout

Layout is the way elements of the design are placed on the page, their position in relation to other things on the page.
When a media presentation is being put together contrast in shape, lines, colour, texture, lettering and size create interest for the reader or viewer.

A Simply Size

1 In these two pictures the sizes have been reversed. What effect does the size difference have?

a) ....

....

....

....

....

b) ....

....

....

....

....

B See-Saw Margery Daw

1 Using a sketch of a see-saw illustrate each of the layout features described below.

a) balanced

b) unbalanced

2 Draw a line through each of the symbols to show each one is balanced.

C Lively Layout

1 Use these elements to sketch a draft layout for a media presentation for your own assessment such as a poster, book cover or CD cover.

appropriate words	dominant image	lines to lead the eye
balance	texture	lettering

Lighting is the arrangement or effect of lights in a presentation or production. Lighting used in specific ways can be used to create special effects.

A Lighting Up

1 Connect the type of light with its function by drawing an arrow between the two.

	Type	Function
a)	Spotlights	For general illumination of an area.
b)	Striplights	Controlled light focused in one area
c)	Floodlights	A row of coloured lights for general illumination.

2 What type of lighting would you select for the introduction of your presentation and what is the reason for this choice?

....
....
....
....
....

B Lighting Matters

1 When a lighting technician uses these techniques what effect is achieved?

a) Colour filters : ....
....
....
....

b) Back light : ....
....
....
....

c) Fill light : ....
....
....
....

C Keeping the Interest Going

1 How could the set and lighting contribute to your dramatic or film presentation? Write four points in each list.

Stage Set	Lighting
a)	a) ....
b)	b) ....
c)	c) ....
d)	d) ....

Elements

The elements of a media or dramatic presentation are the basic parts that constitute the whole.

A Understanding Text

1 Write a brief definition for each of these elements.

a) Title Page ....

b) Blurb ....

c) Author Information ....

d) Bibliography ....

2 Match these terms with their definitions by drawing an arrow between the two.

a)	extract	a conversation featured in a book, play or film.
b)	quote	a selected passage from a text
c)	dialogue	to do with spoken (or written) words.
d)	verbal	a passage or statement repeated from a text

B Media Material

1 Unscramble the words listed to find the elements used in media presentation.

a) l i t t e g a e p ....
b) p r a g s h i c ....
c) r e b a n n ....
d) g r a b n o d u c k ....
e) o n f t ....
f) u m e n r a b ....
g) k i n l s ....
h) L U R ....
i) l e d h a e i n ....
j) g e s m i a ....

2 There are two important techniques that must be included when producing a web page or static image.

a) .... techniques.
b) .... techniques.

C See and Say Wordsearch

1 In this wordsearch there are nine visual and nine verbal techniques to be found. Circle them in the wordsearch then list them in the columns under the appropriate heading. Look in every direction.

Visual	Verbal
....	....
....	....
....	....
....	....
....	....
....	....
....	....
....	....
....	....

E	V	O	I	C	E	O	V	E	R	M
X	F	O	N	T	V	E	C	I	O	V
P	I	C	T	U	R	E	S	N	R	G
R	C	O	L	O	U	R	O	A	S	N
E	E	S	I	S	U	L	B	H	N	I
S	S	T	A	L	O	E	A	V	O	R
S	U	U	E	G	D	P	R	B	I	E
I	A	M	U	I	E	E	S	E	T	T
O	P	E	S	L	O	B	M	Y	S	T
N	A	R	R	A	T	I	O	N	E	E
G	N	I	T	H	G	I	L	A	U	L
S	N	O	I	T	A	T	O	U	Q	L

Language is communication that uses words. The use of a language device should aid communication and add interest to a piece of writing.

A Wonderful Words

1 When constructing a media or dramatic presentation the understanding of the ways language may be used is an advantage. Revise your understanding of language devices by completing this chart with a definition and two examples for each.

	Device	Definition	Two Examples
a)	pun	....	a) *Smart cookies don't burn* b) ......
b)	hyperbole	....	a) ...... b) ......
c)	ambiguity	....	a) ...... b) ......
d)	neologism	....	a) ...... b) ......
e)	cliche	....	a) ...... b) ......
f)	jargon	....	a) ...... b) ......
g)	slang	....	a) ...... b) ......
h)	colloquialism	....	a) ...... b) ......
i)	simile	....	a) ...... b) ......
j)	metaphor	....	a) *Tom is a lion when protecting his children.* b) ......
k)	alliteration	....	a) ...... b) ......

140 Vocalisation

Vocalisation is the manner in which a sound or word is spoken. A performer breathes life into a performance by vocalising.

A Understanding Differences

1 Explain some differences between each of the following.

a) Written language and spoken language.

....

....

....

....

....

b) Scripted talk and impromptu speech.

....

....

....

....

....

B Actor's Advice

1 Place the listed words in the spaces in this paragraph

attentive	phrases	conviction
natural	experimenting	images
performer	unlearnt	purposefully

A .... needs to know what to say, and find how to say it by .... with the words, the .... and the .... he or she wants the audience to receive. The aim is for the speech to sound .... and .... The words should be delivered with .... and confidence so that those who are listening are .... and interested from the start. A media or dramatic presentation should be delivered ....

C Vocal Delivery

1 When delivering a performance each of the following vocal terms needs to be considered. Write a brief definition beneath each term.

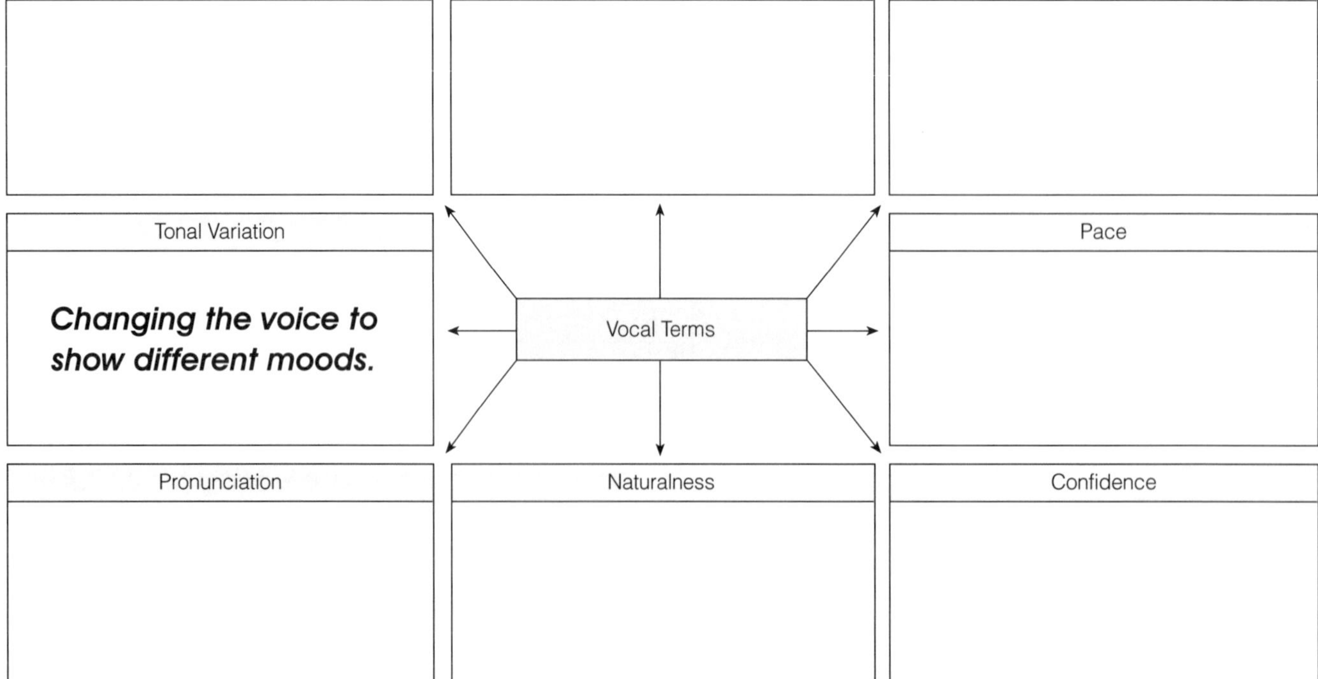

Music

Music in a media presentation sets the mood, affects the emotions or prepares the audience for something that is to happen.

A Music to the Ears

1 Explain how music could be incorporated into each of the following media or drama presentations.

a) An interview :

....

....

....

....

b) A monologue :

....

....

....

....

c) A demonstration :

....

....

....

....

B Background Music

1 The range of music available is very wide. What would be the most suitable background music to consider for each of the following presentations?

a) A romantic scene from a text.

....

....

b) War poetry.

....

....

c) A scene full of tension from a play.

....

....

d) A futuristic scene from a film.

....

....

e) Interview with a troubled character.

....

....

C Making Music

1 You have been asked to include music to accompany your presentation.

What kind of music would be suitable for your topic? ....

....

....

Where would it be played? ....

....

....

Why have you chosen this particular type of music? ....

....

....

....

....

....

Sound Effects

Sound Effects are sounds other than speech or music made artificially for use in a play, film or dramatic presentation. Recordings of various sounds are available on CD's, tapes and on the internet.

A Balloon Blowing

1 Blow up a balloon and see how many different sounds you are able to create. List them in this area.

B Making Sound Effects

1 Rather than use the recordings already available devise some sound effects from material available at home or in the classroom. Be inventive.

Material Used	Sound Effect

C Sound and Mood

1 Directors may use sound to evoke a particular mood. It makes the setting and atmosphere more realistic. What kind of mood and environment do these sounds suggest? One has been completed for you.

	Sound	Mood	Environment
a)	wind howling		
b)	laughing children		
c)	bells tolling		
d)	running water	*nature, peace*	*trout fishing, bush walking*
e)	car horns		

2 Continue this exercise in the same way with sounds that would be suitable to include in your production.

	Sound	Mood	Environment
a)			
b)			
c)			
d)			

Headlines

Headlines are used to attract the eye to the article or media item. To hold the attention it must have impact.
Puns and alliteration are language devices that are often used in headlines, e.g. *Tennis Players Toss In Game*
Troubled Tennis Tournament Terminated

A Clever Lines

1 From each of the following sources find a headline that has impact by using language in an interesting way.

a) Newspaper :

....

....

b) Magazine :

....

....

c) Poster :

....

....

d) CD cover :

....

....

B Hot Headlines

1 Create some pun-based headlines of your own for these sports.

a) Rugby :

....

....

b) Yachting :

....

....

c) Snowboarding :

....

....

d) Cricket :

....

....

e) .... : (own choice)

....

....

C Header Page

1 Draft a preliminary idea for a web page headline section. Choose a website for anything you like but make your design eye-catching so that someone surfing the net would be persuaded to stay and fully investigate the site.

Balance

Balance is when different elements are equal, evenly placed or in the correct proportions visually.

A Eye Up

1 Place a line through each figure to show symmetry or balance. There are many options but choose one line only

a) circle

b) square

c) rectangle

d) triangle

2 Circle the designs that show true balance in their formation.

a) b) c) d) e)

B Having an Eye For It

People who have been taught to read scan any page from left to right across the page and from top to bottom. Keep this in mind when organising the placement and balance of your compositions.

1 Tick the pages that show balance in their compositions.

a) b) c) d) e) f)

Happy Birthday

C Eye-Catching

1 Draft a design for a flyer to advertise the text you are studying. The design must include some feature showing balance.
[✓ Checkpoint in answers]

Page Components

Page components are all the parts that make up a web page.

A Doing Its Job

1 What is the function of each of the following components from an internet web page?

a) Text ....

....

b) Hyperlinks ....

....

c) Icons ....

....

d) Graphic ....

....

e) Banner ....

....

f) Fonts ....

....

B Bold Fonts

1 Complete each of these statements about what needs to be considered when constructing a good web site.

a) A web site should be made with a .... purpose.

b) A web page should be attractive and .... in design.

c) The page should .... in terms of its purpose.

d) It should be easy to .... from one page to another.

e) A good website should be fast to ....

C My Own Web Page

1 Devise a basic layout for a web page on a sport or hobby in which you participate. Make sure all the components are placed and labelled clearly in the frame provided.

Character Overview

A character is a person in a novel, play or film. A character overview is a summary of a character.

A Character Statistics

1 Using an important character from a text being studied, develop a character overview using the following headings.

a) Text being studied : ....

....

b) Writer : ....

c) Character's name : ....

d) Character's age : ....

e) Physical description : ....

....

....

f) Occupation : ....

g) Immediate family : ....

....

....

h) Interests : ....

....

....

....

B Personal Characteristics

1 Using the same character selected in A write brief notes on him or her under these headings.

a) Attitudes to life : ....

....

....

....

b) Opinions held : ....

....

....

....

c) General personality : ....

....

....

....

d) Key catch-phrases used : ....

....

....

....

C Get the Picture

1 Around this silhouette make notes about a character chosen from another text being studied. Try to cover all the points mentioned above as well as their speech, costume, props required, and music where relevant.

[✓ Checkpoint in answers]

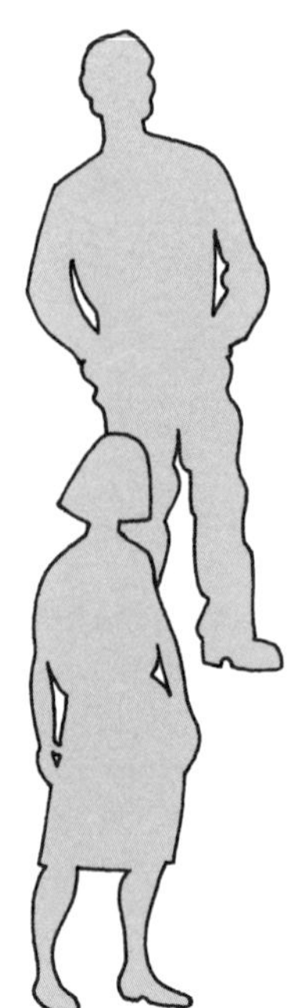

Dialogue from Text

Dialogue from text is the spoken words of characters.

A Analysing an Incident

1 Choose an incident from a text being studied on which to base a performance. Answer each question that follows.

a) What are the names of those involved?

....

b) What situation led up to the incident?

....

c) What was the incident that had such an impact on you?

....

d) What was the resolution to the incident?

....

B Role Play

1 In an interview presentation involving an important character from a text being studied, what are the requirements of the dialogue for each of the following?

a) The Interviewer

....

b) The Character

....

C Scripting the Start

1 Write the introductory section of your script that 'sets the scene' for the audience so they understand how the incident evolved. You have only two actors in the scene.

....

You may have to continue on refill.

Costume

Costume is a set of clothes worn by an actor or performer for a role. Costumes range from very elaborate period dress to the simplest of costumes which are little more than small additions to everyday attire.

A Cool vs Nerd

1 Make notes of simple adjustments of uniform and general appearance (plus props) that could turn this schoolboy into a 'nerdish' character.

....
....
....
....
....
....
....
....
....
....
....

B Building a Costume

1 What three simple costume additions could be made to a student playing one of these characters?

a) A farmer ....
....
....

b) A pirate ....
....
....

c) A baby ....
....
....

d) A detective ....
....
....

C Simple is Best

1 Choose one of the characters from a text being studied and devise a simple costume for a student playing the part. Indicate any physical features that need to be altered by make-up. Write notes to accompany your sketch.

....
....
....
....
....
....
....
....
....
....
....
....
....
....

A drama set is the area where actors perform and includes the arrangement of the stage furnishings.

A Stage Geography

The actors have a stage area to perform in and this is divided up into specific regions. The technical terms applied to these areas are used by directors in theatre.

1 Label this stage area with the correct technical terms listed below.

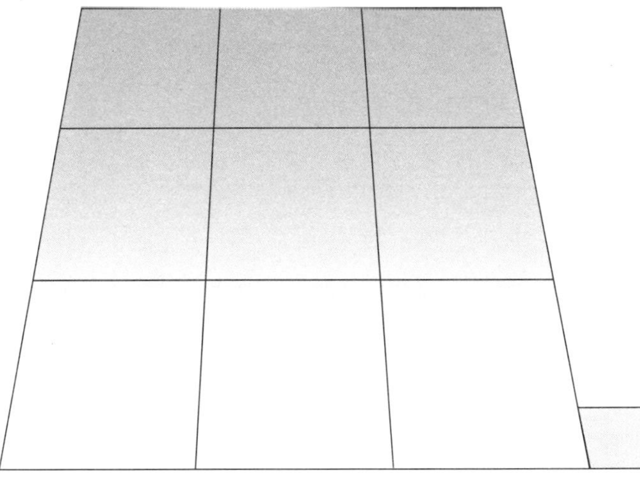

Upstage	downstage	prompt corner
centre (C)	stage left	stage right
up centre (U.C.)	right (R)	down centre (D.C.)
audience	down left (D.L.)	up right (U.R.)
left (L)	down right (D.R.)	up left (U.L.)

B Simple Sets

The script for a performance may be enhanced by the addition of simple stage furnishings, props or rostra. Often a simple set can be more effective as it allows the audience to contribute with their imagination.

1 For the presentation of an incident from a text being studied, list only the MOST essential requirements needed by the actor/s onstage.

a) Incident to be presented : ....

....

....

....

....

....

b) Essential stage furnishings : ....

....

....

....

....

....

....

C Stage Set-Up

1 For a performance in front of your class of an incident from a text being studied, make preliminary sketches of the simple stage set you will require. Limit the stage rostra, lighting, chairs, tables, etc, to those that can be set out with the minimum of fuss.

a) Floor plan of set (Bird's-eye view)

Stage Front

b) Perspective plan of set

Stage Front

Achievement Standard 1.8 - Test 1

Write about a media presentation developed from a text you have studied in class.

Choose one question. Write about 200 words. Support your points with specific details gathered from the text.

1 Describe the key idea behind the media presentation developed. Why was this key idea important?

OR 2 Describe the components of the media presentation you have developed. Why are these components important?

OR 3 Describe the verbal techniques you have used. How have you made them appealing?

OR 4 Choose several visual techniques you have used and show how they are important to the overall design. You could choose from colour, graphics, shape, lines, texture, lettering, symbolism, layout, special effects.

You may need to continue on refill.

Achievement Standard 1.8 - Test 2

Write about a dramatic presentation developed from a text you have studied in class.

Choose one question. Write about 200 words. Support your points with specific details from the text.

	1	Describe the important character you choose to present. Explain why he/she is important.
OR	2	Describe a critical moment the character was involved in. Why was this moment critical?
OR	3	Identify key ideas about the character. Explain the techniques you used to present these ideas in a dramatic way.
OR	4	Describe several key events or challenges involving the character. Explain how they affect or involve that person.
OR	5	Identify specific techniques you have used to present your character. What are the reasons you have used them?

You may need to continue on refill.

Choosing a Topic

Be careful with your choice of topic. It is important to choose one which interests you and one where a wide range of resources is readily available.

A What is Interesting?

1 Circle any of the topics below that have some interest for you as a Year 11 student.

a) A famous New Zealander.

b) An aspect of local history.

c) A threatened species.

d) Pacific Island customs.

e) Indigenous crafts.

f) Protocol on the marae.

g) S.A.D.D.

h) Local musicians.

i) Conservation or pollution?

j) Extreme sports.

B What Interests Me?

1 List ten research topics that are New Zealand-based and you find interesting enough to follow up. Consider all cultures, historical events, lifestyles of eras, famous people and issues.

a) ....

b) ....

c) ....

d) ....

e) ....

f) ....

g) ....

h) ....

i) ....

j) ....

C Refining the Choice

1 From A or B choose the topic that has the most appeal to you and write it in the rectangle.

a) The topic I have chosen is : [ ]

b) I think this would be interesting because ....

....

....

c) Some areas I could follow up on this topic are ....

....

....

....

....

....

d) To do this research I could take the following broad steps

1. Make a list of key words likely to help when trying to find material.

2. ....

....

3. ....

....

Each step of the research process needs to be recorded from the very beginning. It is important to keep a dated log of each step as it is completed. This will help to keep you focused and to complete each stage in an orderly manner. The log should begin with the date the research assignment is set and end with the date the assignment is due, so that the time available is well organised.

A Time Guide

1 A time guide will keep you on time in your research. By keeping to it your assignment will be handed in on time and you will avoid failing the Standard because of lateness. Use these headings (as well as your own) to design a Research Time Guide in the space provided below. Tasks which take longer should be begun first e.g. requesting books from the National Library.

Research Topic :

Work Plan :

Week 1 : 3 periods
Week 2 : 3 periods
Week 3 : 3 periods

Assignment begun :

Assignment due :

[✓ Checkpoint in answers]

B Research Headings

1 Design your own personal dated research log heading. It may include some of the following: start date, steps taken, resources used and completion date.

154 Brainstorming

Brainstorming is the first step towards producing a written report. Brainstorming involves recognising what you already know about a topic, thinking about what you need to find out and developing some key words to help focus your research efforts.

A My Topic

1a) Write the name of the research topic you have chosen for your class assignment.

....

b) Who is the audience for this work? ....

B A Storming Start

1 Follow these steps in the brainstorming process. Use the research topic you have chosen for presentation.

What I already know

What I want to find out

Possible graphics to be found or created

Key words give the focus you need to find information on the topic. They are the names, terms and concepts to do with your topic. They also help to keep you focused when gathering information.

A Looking Carefully

1 Look at the brainstorming idea shown below and circle the six key words (hint : they would make suitable headings.)

volcanic islands
pendants
carvings
printed designs
houses
deep valleys
wind
fish
tapa
currents
rich decoration
lashed beams
circular in shape
food
plaited fabrics

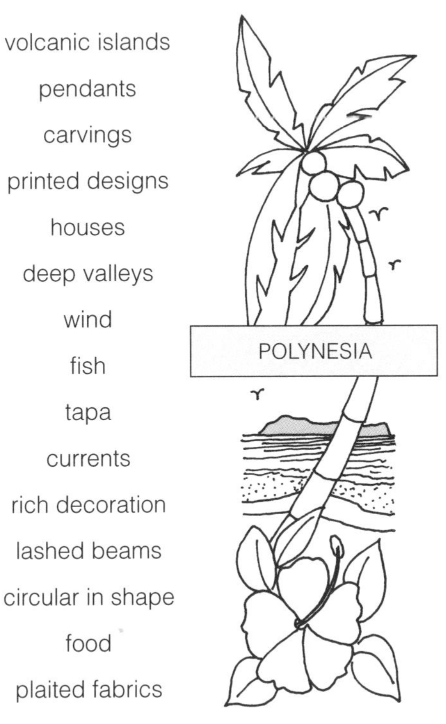

canoes
geography
stars
open-sided
coconut
alluvial plains
breadfruit
art
stone images
clothing
thatched roofs
bananas
coral atolls
tattooing
navigation

B Sorting Words

1 Using the six key words found in A as headings, sort the rest of the words into boxes. There are four words per heading.

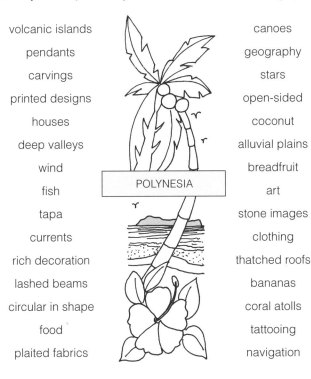

C Terrible Taniwha

1 Highlight the key words in the passage below.

Taniwha, the spirits of the water, not only live in the ocean but are found in rivers, lakes and underground. Many arrived from Hawaiiki, as told in Maori legend, as guardians of ancestral canoes and of the people who travelled in these waka. Taniwha generally lived in caves, deep pools or near rapids in rivers. Most taniwha behaved well with the people with whom they were associated but they could be spiteful and malicious when others disturbed them, often devouring any intruder. At their death the taniwha's bones may become an island, reef or rock.

D Food for the Brain

1 In the brain diagram place the name of your topic in the centre then quickly note as many key words, ideas and facts about it as you can.

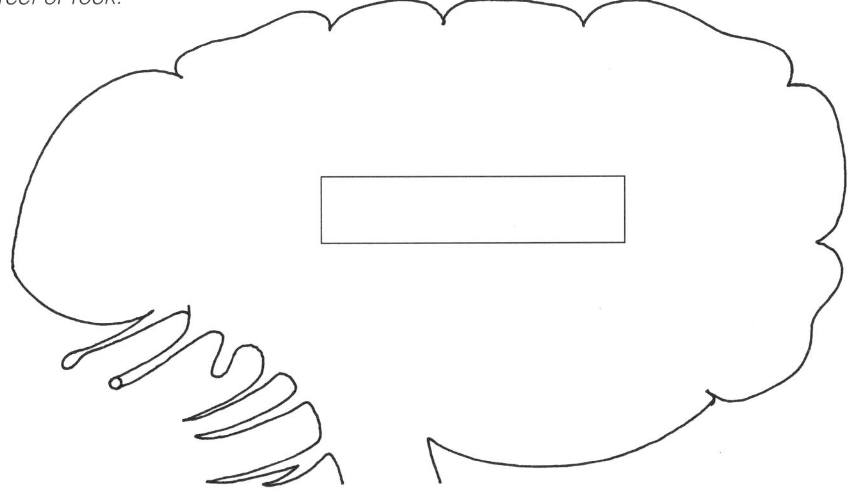

Key Questions

It is important to narrow the focus of your research to five or six key questions. Use the What? Where? When? Who? Why? and How? questions to help. It is important to ask open questions as these will provide more information.

A Open or Closed Questions?

1 Label each question **O** for an open question or **C** for a closed question.

a) How are we polluting our environment? ☐

b) When did Captain Cook arrive in New Zealand? ☐

c) Does a Kiwi have feathers or hair? ☐

d) Why is conservation crucial to our future? ☐

e) How does violence on television influence the young? ☐

f) What problems do new immigrants face in New Zealand? ☐

g) Have my family always lived in New Zealand? ☐

h) What role did the Maori Battalion play in World War II? ☐

i) Is my culture significant to me? ☐

j) Is the 'Buzzy Bee' a New Zealand icon? ☐

B Finding Out

1 What is it that you wish to find out from your research efforts? Write three open questions on your class research topic.

a) ....

b) ....

c) ....

2 Write three closed questions on your research topic.

a) ....

b) ....

c) ....

C Opening Up Your Topic

1 For each of these kinds of information source, write one or two open questions for your own research topic that you could follow up.

a) Written sources: ....

b) Oral sources: ....

c) Visual sources: ....

[✓ Checkpoint in answers]

Sources of information can be written, visual or oral. You can find information at school, at home and in your local community or you can investigate national or international sources such as the internet.

A Collecting Information

1 Place each source of information in the most suitable segment. After you have placed the sources into the diagram, colour-code them according to where you might find them (at home = blue, at school = yellow, local community = green, national = red, international = purple.)

teachers	reference books	head offices	family members	encyclopaedia
websites	internet	magazines	school library	interviews
National Library	students	subject specialists	official sources	posters
local organisations	Encarta	central organisations	surveys	newspapers
school archives	pamphlets	public library	maps	local experts
microfiche	television	Year Book	letters	vertical files

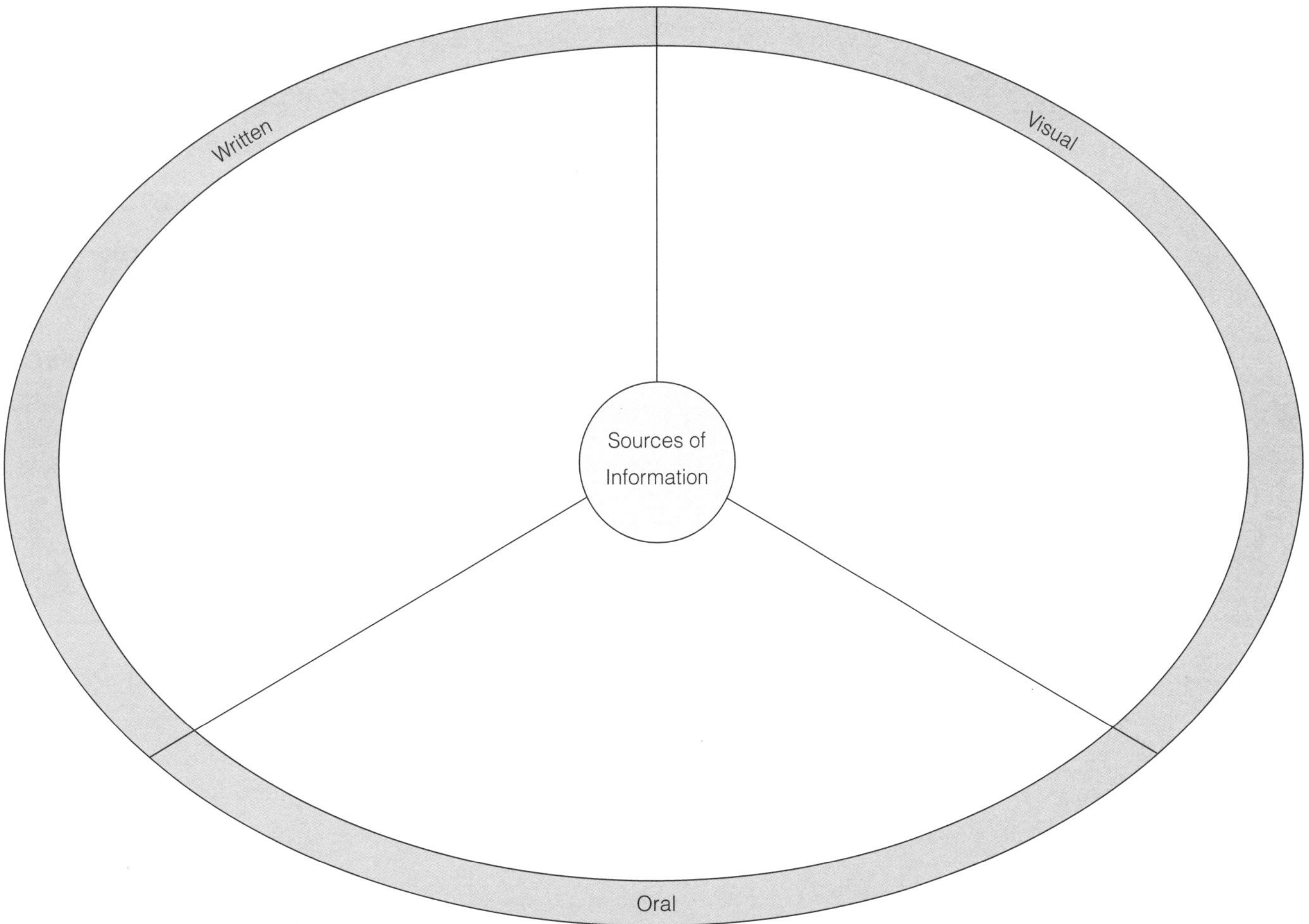

2 Add any further ideas of your own to each segment of the circle after you have listed them here.

....

....

....

158 Bibliography

It is important to record your sources and the information gathered in an acceptable format. A bibliography which records a list of sources used and their authors as well as other details specific to the work being researched is valuable. A bibliography is added at the end and is in alphabetical order acknowledging the author first.

A Defining a Term

1 Use a dictionary to find a definition for each of the following words.

Word	Definition
source	
format	
bibliography	
author	
publisher	

B Website Visits

1 The information below may be used to record websites visited in your bibliography. This exercise is completed for you as an example. Complete one yourself for practice.

Research topic : ***"Surviving the Big OE"***

Site address : ***www.govt.nz/en/home/***

Site creator/owner :

State Services Commission for the New Zealand Government

Menu pathways used to locate research material on the site :

Things to know when . . . . >

Passports and visas >

Get or extend a NZ passport >

Application for a NZ passport

Titles of pages downloaded : ***[pdf. file]***

'Application form for a NZ passport'

C Record to Remember and Remember to Record

1 Make a record of the books or publications from which you have obtained information. As you use the materials update the record. Record author's surname first then initials or first name.

BIBLIOGRAPHY				
Author	Name / Title / URL of Source	Publisher	Place	Year

It is important to gather research information from a variety of sources which include : ❒ Written sources ❒ Oral sources ❒ Visual sources.

Written sources available for research are all the usual resources you would find in a library such as non-fiction books and reference books, as well as newspapers, magazines, pamphlets, brochures and leaflets. Many libraries now provide the option to print out electronic information.

A Research Resources

1 Make a list of ten sources of written material which may be useful for your research project.

a) ....
b) ....
c) ....
d) ....
e) ....
f) ....
g) ....
h) ....
i) ....
j) ....

B The Written Word

1 Define the following terms that refer to written sources available for research.

Term	Definition
archives	
microfiche	
website	
vertical file	

C Terms Finder

1 In the wordsearch you will find the sources that match these descriptions.

a) Imaginative writing ....
b) Factual writing ....
c) Inventor of decimal classification system ....
d) Books used only in library ....
e) Disk storing huge amounts of information ....
f) Lists words alphabetically ....
g) Contains maps ....
h) Annual statistical publication ....
i) Gives annual information on calendar, tide, sun and moon times

....

j) Uses keywords for easy searching on computers

....

D	I	C	T	I	O	N	A	R	Y
A	E	K	O	O	B	R	A	E	Y
T	R	W	E	C	O	R	D	F	A
A	L	L	E	T	H	E	I	E	C
B	N	F	S	Y	O	N	R	R	D
A	M	A	A	T	I	O	O	E	R
S	N	F	L	O	U	I	N	N	O
E	D	I	T	N	Y	T	O	C	M
A	L	M	A	N	A	C	U	E	R
O	W	N	W	O	R	I	D	S	X
N	O	I	T	C	I	F	N	O	N

2 The left-over letters give some advice. The advice is : ....

....

Oral Sources

Oral sources available for research include interviews, radio programmes and speeches.

A Face to Face

1 Mark with a ✓ the oral sources you have used, or plan to use, in your research.

a) A family member ☐
b) A teacher ☐
c) An expert ☐
d) A librarian ☐
e) A witness ☐
f) Radio programme ☐
g) Speech ☐
h) Your class ☐
i) Tapes ☐
j) Video ☐

B Collecting Information

1 A survey is one way to find out what people think about an issue.

a) What is a survey?

A survey is ....

....

....

....

2 Match up the two halves, by drawing an arrow between them to show ways in which a survey can be made worthwhile.

a) Include a fairly	randomly
b) Conclusions should be	large group of people
c) Choose people	carefully worded
d) Questions should be	drawn from survey results

C Graphing Information

1 Once the survey has been completed how can it be presented? Label the following methods of graphing information.

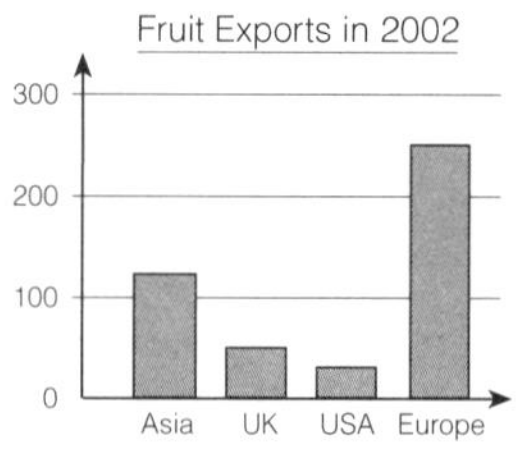

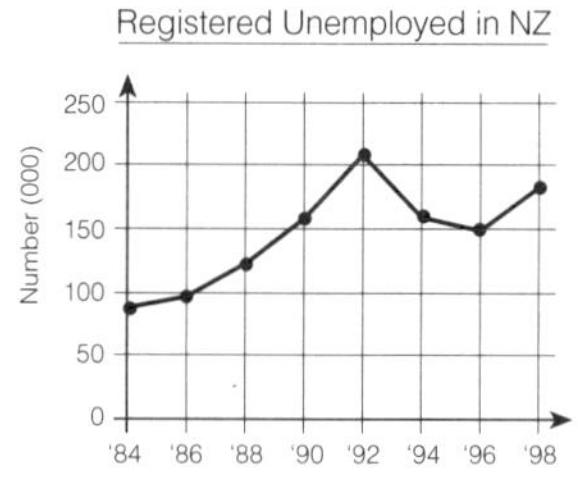

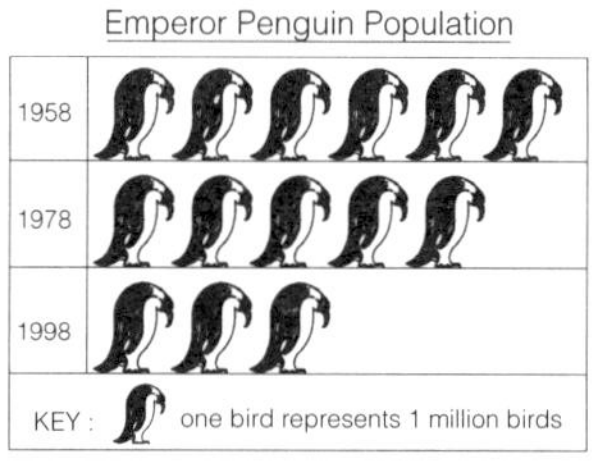

a) .... b) .... c) .... d) ....

D Groundwork for Interviews

1 Preparation for an interview is important. Using the subheadings given, note two things that should be done prior to the interview.

a) Planning before the interview

....

....

b) Planning the questionnaire

....

....

c) Setting up the interview

....

....

d) Getting permission to

....

....

2 Once the interview is over, thanks are given for ....

....

Visual sources that may provide information for research are films, Encarta, electronic sources, videos, television as well as posters and billboards. When researching it is wise to gather information from a variety of sources to gain a broad understanding of the subject from a range of perspectives.

A The Seeing Eye

1 List three visual sources other than those given above.

a) ....

b) ....

c) ....

2 Make a list of the visual sources used during your own research.

....

....

....

....

B At My Fingertips

1 Of the visual sources used by you which one was the most useful and why?

The most useful source was ....

....

because ....

....

....

....

....

....

....

C Library Research

1 Place the following steps used to research a topic into the most logical order.

a) Use the computer catalogue and list available books. ....

b) Brainstorm what you already know ....

c) Make notes from all available sources. ....

d) Check the available books on the shelves. ....

e) Publish and present. ....

f) Select final material required for assignment. ....

g) Choose a research topic. ....

h) Use encyclopedia etc. in the reference section. ....

i) Follow up with other media and sources. ....

j) List key words and search terms. ....

D Visual and Unusual

What was the most unusual visual source you used in your research and what useful information did you gather from it?

....

....

....

....

....

Selecting Information

It is important to select only the information that answers the key questions. Key words help to focus the search on what is relevant.

A Sorting Stuff

1 Using your own research topic, fill in the following chart with relevant details that will narrow down the information to support the three key questions.

Topic : ....

	Written Source	Oral Source	Visual Source
Three Key Questions			
Key Words Used			
Sources Used [✓ Checkpoint in answers]			
Information Sourced			

Drawing a conclusion is making a final statement about how true and important the ideas you have presented are.

A I Have Concluded That . . .

1 What inference do you draw from each of these statements?

a) *'The Buzzy Bee is a New Zealand icon and every child should have possessed one in infancy.'*

....

....

....

b) *'The natural resources of the New Zealand coastline are being decimated with no thought of the future.'*

....

....

....

c) *'Old Man's Beard, an ornamental vine, has a stranglehold on even the tallest trees in the bush.'*

....

....

....

B Finely Defined

1 Use a dictionary to help you write a definition for each of these things which should be found in your research report.

a) Judgement : ....

....

....

b) Generalisation : ....

....

....

c) Conclusion : ....

....

....

d) Deduction : ....

....

....

e) Inference : ....

....

....

C In Conclusion . . .

1 What conclusions have you drawn for each of the key questions asked in your own research topic (see page 162)?

Question 1 ....

Conclusion drawn : ....

....

....

Question 2 ....

Conclusion drawn : ....

....

....

Question 3 ....

Conclusion drawn : ....

....

....

Drafting

Drafting is organising the information gathered in researching your key questions and expressing it in your own words.

A Writing For Myself

1 Write a paragraph using the following information.

Moeraki Boulders

South Island east coast, 60 million years old
cannonball shape, 2 tonne, 2 metre spheres, vary in size
prehistoric bones, shells inside, formed in sea-floor sediments,
part of Maori legend.

....

....

....

....

....

....

....

....

....

....

B In Your Own Words

1 Place suitable words in this passage about expressing research material in your own words.

There is no point in .... material exactly from the text when writing a research assignment. It is important that every step of the .... engages the brain. The more information that is collected from the wide variety of .... that are available, the easier it is to .... then write or word process into a final copy. During these processes of ...., generalisations on particular issues may be drawn and judgements and conclusions linked to the research .... may be made by the student. These should be .... in the draft to indicate a thorough understanding of the research topic.

C Linking Up

1 For the three key questions from page 162, write draft sentences giving the information that answers those questions.

Question 1 ....

....

....

....

Question 2 ....

....

....

....

Question 3 ....

....

....

....

Presenting A Written Report

A written report is the culmination of your research. It should include judgements, conclusions and generalisations you have made when considering the information you have researched.

A Following the Steps

To produce a quality report you must follow the research process outlined on previous pages and fully record the information.

1 Match up the two halves by drawing an arrow between them to show the research process that must be followed to produce a good quality report.

a) Choose a topic	ideas, suitable information and sources.
b) Devise a series of	information relevant to key questions
c) Brainstorm a range of	key questions to research
d) Sources should cover	the report
e) Collect and record	written, visual and oral areas
f) Write up	that interests you

B Research Rulz

1 Complete these sentences with the requirements stated in the research assignment.

a) Teachers must see records of :

- ❒ ....
- ❒ ....
- ❒ ....

b) Templates are provided for :

- ❒ ....
- ❒ ....
- ❒ ....

c) Students must always be aware of :

- ❒ ....
- ❒ ....
- ❒ ....

C Aiming For Excellence

1 Tick off each of these if you have met these steps as mentioned in the marking criteria.

Descriptors

Planning	
❒ States topic	
❒ Poses key questions	
❒ Identifies possible sources	

Information	
❒ Collects	
❒ Selects	
❒ Records in accepted format	

Research Process	
❒ Records steps taken	

Final Report	
❒ Organises	
❒ Presents succinctly	
❒ Makes generalisations	
❒ Forms judgements	

Achievement Standard 1.9 - Test

Analyse this extract from a final report. Make critical comments based on the descriptors listed on page 165. You may mark the text and use the right hand area of this page to make notes.

The decade of jazz and song known as the Roaring Twenties was a time when life appeared to be given over to an existence of little responsibility. From interviews, newspapers, film and other sources I wanted to find out if this assumption was true.

After World War 1 (1914 - 1918), which was a grim period for all the countries involved, the promises made at the Versailles Peace Conference assuring that there would be no more war for at least 50 or 100 years seemed a release for people after the dark times.

Women, who had during the war years shouldered many of the jobs previously done by men, such as farming, factory work and generally taking on responsibilities previously denied them, would not contemplate reverting to a life restricted to 'a woman's place is in the home'. They had tasted freedom. The Roaring Twenties reflected this freedom in short haircuts, loose fitting dresses with above-the-knee skirts, smoking and drinking in public as well as participating in sport and travel to countries far from home. However the 'freedom' for women was balanced with occupations such as office work, attending university, nursing, teaching and generally working outside the home in increasing numbers to provide a better lifestyle.

Those men who returned from the Great War found a different world from the one they left. It was harder to find employment because the countries involved in fighting had to rebuild their economies and had little money with which to pay wages. The Twenties heralded better times and it was a time when men danced the Charleston, wore Oxford bags and drove motor cars which continued to replace the horse and cart. The era also was a time of increased employment and a building boom in houses and commercial premises in cities that were expanding rapidly. Countries once locked in war were gradually opened up to trade and there was a sense of prosperity and good times for everyone.

What assessment would this student earn in your estimation and why? Assessment ....

Reasons : ....

....

....

....

....

Page 4 - Starting the Process

A1* student's own answers

B1* student's own answers

Page 5 - Intended Audience

A1 a) T b) A c) C d) C
e) T f) A g) T h) A
i) C

B1* a) "Some creep has taken my new school shoes! What a dirty scumbag! I'll tear them apart if I find out who nicked them."
b) "Please, Sir. Someone has taken a new pair of school shoes from my bag while we were at P.E."

B2* a) Slang - creep, scumbag, nicked. Short sharp sentences. Angry tone. Cliche - "I'll tear them apart."
b) Formal address. "Please, Sir."
Longer sentence in a statement form.
* examples only - student's own answers

C1* student's own answers
✓ Checkpoint : Adult - *For adult audiences, slang words like 'wagging' and 'freaked' should be avoided or put in inverted commas.*

Page 6 - Purpose of Writing

A1* a) menacing b) sympathetic c) humorous
d) student's own answer

B1* student's own answers
✓ Checkpoint : b) - *Young writers often use too many adjectives. Where you have used two together, cross out the weaker one.*

C1 Favourable :
b) famished, ravenous
c) slender, slim
d) destroy, eliminate
e) intoxicated
Unfavourable :
b) greedy, gluttonous
g) emaciated, scrawny
h) massacre, slaughter
i) inebriated, wasted

Page 7 - Point of View

A2 a) newspaper reporter b) spectator
c) player d) referee
e) ambulance medic f) radio announcer
g) TV commentator h) sports photographer
i) injured player j) coach

B1 a) Jack b) His mother
c) Someone who knows what each character is thinking.

C1 Is told by . . . - 1st person narrative
Is told of the . . . - 2nd person narrative
Gives an . . . - 3rd person narrative
Sees into each . . . - omniscient 3rd person

C2* student's own answers
✓ Checkpoint : b) *There should be a phrase that shows your attitude e.g. 'I'd love to . . .' or 'too dangerous'.*

Page 8 - First-Person Narrative

A1 a) I, my b) I, I, my c) me
d) I, my

B1 The circled personal pronouns and possesive adjectives are as follows (in order):
I, I, myself, my, me, I, my, I, me, I, I, my

C1* student's own answers

D1* student's own answers
✓ Checkpoint : *There should be two tenses (present and past) used in your writing e.g. 'I remember when I was five'.*

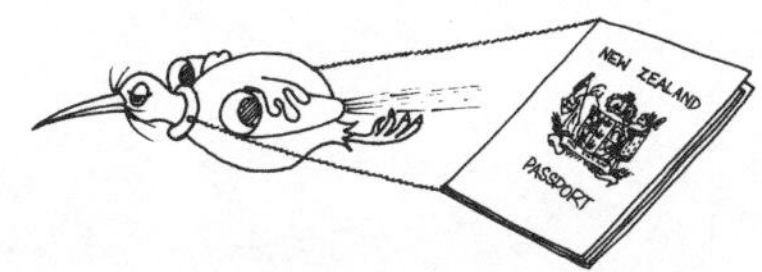

Page 9 - Second-Person Narrative

A1 a) you, I, you b) you, She, her
c) they, I, her

B1 The circled different pronouns are as follows (in order):
You, your, I, me, we.

C1* student's own answers
✓ Checkpoint : *You should have used the word 'you' more times than you used the word 'I'.*

D1 Your horse, Kit, always stood quietly while he waited for you. I have seen him turn his head in your direction, toss his mane and stamp his feet while you chatted with friends. He was the most patient animal and obviously thought you were wonderful. You were lucky to have had such a quiet and gentle friend.

Page 10 - Third-Person Narrative

A1 Suitable pronouns are as follows (in order):
He, his, he, his, his, he, his, him, he, his, his.

B1 The circled personal pronouns are as follows (in order):
he, he, he, they, him, he, himself, he, he.

B2* student's own answers

C1* student's own answer
✓ Checkpoint : *At least one character in your new version of the old story must have changed from winner to loser, or loser to winner.*

Page 11 - The All-Seeing Eye

A1* a) driver, witness, police officer
b) swimmer, surf life-saver, onlooker
c) skier's friend, mountain rescue, doctor
d) team-mate, coach, TV commentator
* examples only - student's own answers

B1* student's own answers
✓ Checkpoint : - *The strongest reaction should be in the writing for the character 'on the receiving end'.*

C1* The writer shows the 'Eye of God' technique by writing what the characters are thinking and feeling. Shirley's heart is pounding and Laura's breath aches as it leaves her lungs. Frankie's thoughts are anxious even while she is running.
* example only - student's own answers

Page 12 - Tone

A1* a) I'm sorry but you have made a mess of all my work.
b) That computer is too slow to do the job required.
c) I will pick up the rubbish but I object because it isn't mine.
d) You are lucky. I would like to go on a trip too.
e) I struggle with mathematics. Algebra is difficult for me.

B1* Excuse me. I think I need to tell you I am tired of you spreading unfounded stories about me. If you don't stop immediately I will take it further.

C1 Favourable : supportive, encouraging, unpretentious, conscientious, sincere.
Unfavourable : aggressive, arrogant, insipid, miserly, conceited.

D1* There is heavy snow, no crowds and this mountain has it all, from beautiful clear runs to gullies, bowls and curving slopes - the day is going to be wonderful. Wait a minute! Whether you are a first-timer or experienced and an efficient downhill skier, take a moment to think safety - mountain safe. * examples only - student's own answers

Page 13 - Setting

A1 a) The arrival of the European people.
b) Start of World War 1.
c) The start of televison services.

B1* student's own answers

C1* student's own answers based on answer from B

Page 14 - Character

A1 a) circled words - sarcastic, overbearing, intimidating, spiteful, cunning.
b) a kindly or pleasant character

B1 Arrogant - haughty, contemptuous, scornful, conceited self-satisfied, supercilious. - others
Spoilt Child - petulant, touchy, whinging, peevish, sulky, sullen. - others
Concerned Parent - anxious, worried, solicitous, sympathetic, uneasy, apprehensive. - others
Fussy - precise, flustered, agitated, perturbed, bustling, exacting. - others

C1* a) calmly, climbable, positive, energy, confident, invigorated, purposefully.
b) apprehensively, intimidating, uncertain, courage, fearful, weak, diffidently.
* examples only - student's own answers

D1 large, bare, wooden, long, baggy, black, thin, white, bony, thin, fine, black, long, own.

Page 15 - Stereotypes

A1 a) Neat, glasses, polished shoes, books in hand
b) Well-built, fit, handsome, friendly to the 'in' crowd, blond
c) Strong make-up, eccentric clothes, rings and bangles

A2 a) Beefy, fit, likes to be with 'the boys', drinks beer, trains hard
b) Lean and focused, has endurance, dedicated
c) Dresses in a suit, briefcase, knowledgeable, reliable

B1* *student's own signals based on the collected material

Page 16 - Events

A1* student's own answers

B1 f) Pack the car, i) Drive to the beach, a) Select a place and unpack the car, d) Change for a swim, j) Surf the waves, b) Lifeguards give shark warning, e) Swimmers and surfers leave water, g) Wait for 'All clear', c) Return to water, h) Repack car to drive home.

C1* Picture A : Looking at snow capped mountain peaks, clear weather, deciding best route.
Picture B : Two on climb. Steep, snow-covered slope, climber hit by falling rocks, knocked unconscious.
Picture C : Climbers return to base camp, injured climber needs help. relief from partner at Base Camp.
* example only - student's own answers

Page 17 - Sentence Length

A1* a) The red car skidded across the gravel road.
b) I picked up the yellow surfboard and ran down the sandy beach to the sparkling waves.
c) High in the cloudless sky a white bird glided.
d) Sarah brushed her black hair in front of the shiny mirror.
e) Tom clambered over the sharp rocks to the mysterious entrance of the cliff cave.
* examples only - student's own answers

B1* student's own answers
✓ Checkpoint : d) *This should be your shortest sentence.*

C1 As you take your seat, harness and belt up, you know this is no ordinary amusement ride. Your mind races and your throat begins to dry, while your heart rate increases dramatically. You wait. The countdown begins. Without further warning you are slingshot skyward in a reclining position. At 160 kph facial muscles are stretched and distorted by the g's.

Page 18 - Dialogue

A1 a) "Where is my bag?" asked Marie.
b) "I've no idea," replied her mother.
c) "I put it by the door," returned Marie, "and someone has moved it."
d) "Don't look at me. I've enough to do," her mother responded.
e) Marie frowned, "Perhaps I've made a mistake."

B1 "By cripes, Wiremu, that's a big eel! Where were you fishing?" asked James.
"Down at the big pool south of the bridge," replied Wiremu.
"Say that's a choice place! I've fished there too, but never caught anything that size."
"Just luck, Bro. Just plain luck."

C1
"Knock, knock."	"Knock, knock."
"Who's there?"	"Who's there?"
"Albert."	"Yah."
"Albert who?"	"Yah who?"
"Albert you'll never guess."	"Ride 'em cowboy!"
"Knock, knock."	"Knock, knock."
"Who's there?"	"Who's there?"
"You."	"Althea."
"You who?"	"Althea who?"
"Did you call?"	"Althea later alligator!"

C2 a) What has been said has speech marks around those words and a comma separates these words from the words that tell who is speaking.
b) Two commas have been used to separate the spoken words which have been divided into two parts.

Page 19 - Rough Drafts

A1* student's own answers
B1* student's own answers
✓ Checkpoint : *Your embarrassment should be highlighted by a physical reaction like a hot blush or a strong emotion word like 'hate' in the writing.*

C1
Across	Always needs . . .	- spelling
	Vary the length . . .	- sentences
	Correct structure . . .	- grammar
	Used to start . . .	- capital letters
	Not to be used . . .	- and
Down	Rules for this . . .	- punctuation
	Completes a . . .	- full stop

Page 20 - Beginning, Middle, End

A1 Beginning - Humpty Dumpty sat on a wall.
Middle - Humpty Dumpty fell off the wall.
End - Humpty Dumpty could not be fixed.
A2* student's own answers based on selected nursery rhyme
B1* a) 'Hinemoa and Tutanekai'
b) Hinemoa and Tutanekai fell in love.
Their love was forbidden.
c) Hinemoa swam to Mokoia Island guided by Tutanekai's flute. She smashed the calabashes of Tutanekai's servant.
d) Tutanekai found Hinemoa in the hot spring and took her as his wife.
* example only - student's own answers

C1 a) Structure your essay with at least three parts.
b) The beginning sets the scene.
c) Sentence beginnings should vary.
d) Paragraphs have a central idea.
e) The middle tells the story.
f) Short sentences quicken the pace.
g) A number of sentences make a paragraph.
h) The end closes the story.
i) Essays should follow a logical order.
j) Long sentences slow the pace.

D1 a) chronological b) variety c) interest
d) details e) logical f) essential

Page 21 - Beginning or Introduction

A1* student's own answers
B1* student's own answers
C1* student's own answers

Page 22 - Middle or Body

A1 a) The body tells the story.
b) Each paragraph presents a further part of the event.
c) Tension and conflict between people can arise.
d) It is best to concentrate on one event.
e) The story builds logically.
f) Use metaphors to colour your writing.
g) Speech must be natural.
B1* student's own answers
✓ Checkpoint : c) *Your answer should show that this conflict ends at this time.*
B2* student's own answers

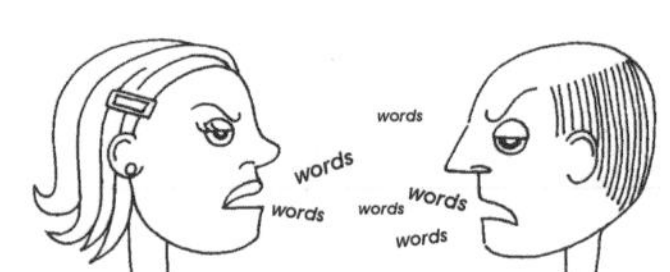

Page 23 - End or Conclusion

A1* student's own answers
B1 a) A bush fire. b) surfing
c) a man d) the bush
C1* student's own answers - various conclusions possible.
✓ Checkpoint : *The conclusion must show the fate of the people in the river i.e. saved or drowned.*

Page 24 - AS 1.1 - Test

* student's own answer
Marking checklist :
a) ideas well expressed
b) ideas develop during story
c) writing style used appropriate
d) material organised well
e) accurate spelling
f) accurate punctuation
g) text correctly paragraphed

✓ Checkpoint : *Count your words. Under 300 and you risk a 'Not Achieved'. If you have written too much you can probably improve impact by cutting. The marker wants quality not quantity.*

Page 25 - What to Write About

A1* a) Bullying in schools.
b) Eliminating sports fees in school.
c) Prefects - a thing of the past.
d) Schools are becoming too large.
e) Drugs in schools.
* examples only - student's own answers
A2* student's own answers
B1* student's own answers
B2* a) Global Warming
b) World Peace - is it possible?
c) The Environment is the World's Wealth
d) Education is the Key to our Future
e) AIDS - still a threat.
* examples only - student's own answers
C1* student's own answers

Page 26 - Gathering Information

A1* School Sources :
library, pupils, teachers, computers, encyclopaedia, non-fiction, video, - others
Local Area Sources :
local newspaper, public library, people (experts, others for opinions), movies, organisations, photographs, radio
National Sources :
newspapers, central organisations, directories, TV (news, documentaries), magazines, films / videos, national library, databases, - others
International Sources :
organisations overseas, newspapers, foreign people, embassies, television, documentaries, latest international research (health, geographical, space), world focused organisations (WHO, Amnesty International), databases, maps, world charities, - others
* examples only - student's own answers

Page 27 - Brainstorming

A1* student's own answers
B1* student's own answers
C1* student's own answers
✓ Checkpoint : *Delete any ideas for which you have no support from hard facts, common sense or actual cases you know of.*

Page 28 - Essay Planning

A1 a) All topics support the issue except 'Ignore getting involved.'
b) All topics support the issue except 'Being 'cool' is the most important.'
B1 a) School - a safe environment.
Talk to someone.
Inform those in the school support system.
Use of teen mediators.
b) Involved teens are successful teens.
Supporting fellow teens
Working as volunteers
Contributing to the family by working
C1* student's own answers
✓ Checkpoint : *Is the most effective point the last on the list?*

Page 29 - Paragraphing

A1 a) Explanation b) Statement
c) Example
A2 a) Statement - All New Zealanders should be aware that the natural elements of our coastline are being depleted rapidly.
b) Explanation - Those who plunder shellfish have no consideration for the ability of the stock to replenish itself.
c) Example - In places like Mt Maunganui a ban has had to be placed on collecting mussels so that the stocks may recover.
* examples only - student's own answers
B1* student's own answers
B2* student's own answers based on B1
B3* student's own answers based on B2
✓ Checkpoint : *Is your final sentence precise enough to be rewarded?'*
School jackets are expensive' - would not be rewarded
'My school jacket cost $80' would be rewarded.

Page 30 - Sentence Construction

A1 a) Sea anemones capture passing prey.
b) Most anemones remain in one place.
c) The wandering anemones move about.
d) Mangroves, rock pools, boulders and reefs provide habitats for anemones.
e) The tentacles bristle with barbs.

A2* a) Species of anemone are to be found on New Zealand coastal beaches.
b) Paralysing barbs can be fatal to small fish.
c) Passing victims may be caught in the anemones tentacles.
d) Small sea creatures avoid the anemone.
* examples only - student's own answers

B1 a) 'They' could mean anemones or shrimps.
b) This sentence gives the impression that anemones live in environments other than the sea.
c) The word neither should have nor with it.
d) It is not clear whether one or a number of anemones can look like a garden.
e) It appears the victims wait for the anemones to kill them.

C1 a) Have
b) Has
c) Is / Was
d) Are / Were
e) Were / Are
f) Was / Is

Page 31 - Introductory Paragraphs

A1* a) How can examinations be fair to all students?
b) I think that everyone who has been faced with an examination has been nervous.
c) People dread the thought of an imminent examination.
d) Examinations should be a thing of the past! Who needs them?
* examples only - student's own answers

B1* a) Formal writing is generally presented from the viewpoint of the writer.
b) Formal writing does not include slang, colloquialisms or abbreviations.
c) Sentences should be grammatical and varied.
d) The opening sentence should grab the attention of the reader and encourage further reading.
* examples only - student's own answers

C1 a) I b) F c) F
d) I e) I f) F
g) F h) F i) I
j) I

C2* student's own answers

✓ Checkpoint : *People who wish to persuade often exaggerate. Rewrite any sentence where you have exaggerated.*

Page 32 - Body of the Essay

A1* a) Generally less cost compared with fashion clothes.
b) No 'what to wear' problems.
c) Identifiable as a school group.
d) Encourages school pride and belonging.

A2* a) Room for individuality.
b) Individual physical shapes better catered for.
c) Freedom from 'cloned' look.
d) Cheaper ranges of clothing now available.
* examples only - student's own answers

B1 a) spelling
b) punctuation
c) grammar
d) sentence structure
e) paragraphing

C1* student's own answers based on selected editorial

Page 33 - Conclusion

A1* student's own answers
B1* student's own answers
C1* student's own answers

✓ Checkpoint : - *The last sentence of your conclusion should contain either a suggested solution to the problem or a prediction of what the long-term consequences may be.*

Page 34 - Formal Diction

A1* a) I am very angry. b) She keeps interfering.
c) He has run away. d) He is a nuisance.
e) She is a nuisance we can do without.
* examples only - student's own answers

B1 John was highly excited at the thought of a holiday with his father as he was very like him. They both enjoyed hunting in the bush, even when it rained very heavily, and they seldom got into trouble. His father had taught him to respect the bush and not behave foolishly, otherwise he could fail or succeed on his past experience.
* example only - student's own answer

C1* student's own answers

✓ Checkpoint : - *The words 'like' or 'as' must be in your similes, must not be in your metaphors and may be in your personifications.*

Page 35 - Syntax

A2 a) The rabbit was introduced to New Zealand for skins and meat.
b) Originally, rainbow trout came from California.
Rainbow trout originally came from California.
Rainbow trout came from California originally.
c) Stoats and weasels are predators on native wildlife.
d) Opossums damage forests, orchards and gardens.
(variations in order of locations possible)

B1* student's own answers
B2* student's own answers

C1 a) simple b) complex c) compound
d) simple e) compound f) complex

Page 36 - Signposts

A1* student's own answers
B1* student's own answers
C1* student's own answers based on work in Ex A.

✓ Checkpoint : *Your first sentence should contain either the exact words of the topic or words that mean exactly the same, e.g. 'the way people of our own age influence us' for c).*

Page 37 - Rough Drafts

A1* student's own answers

✓ Checkpoint : - *Your readers will respond better to you if you use some slang, but it must be used in a controlled way for effect. Allow yourself two examples.*

B1* student's own answers based on their article from Ex A
C1* student's own answers based on criteria in Ex B

Page 38 - Rewriting

A1 student's own answers based on article rough draft Pg 37

✓ Checkpoint : - *Essay jargon creates a bad impression; rewrite any words like 'introduction', 'essay', 'paragraph' and 'conclusion' that are in your first draft.*

B1 The secret to achieving good writing is to scribble a first draft regardless of quality and then revise and revise until quality emerges.

C1 a) The opening paragraph should 'hook' the reader's attention.
b) The conclusion should be as strong as the introduction.
c) Proofreading includes all the writing conventions.
C2 interesting, accurate, clear, concise
C3 Choose an essay topic you know something about.

Page 39 - Spelling

A1&2 constantely - constantly; there - their; litering - littering; presense - presence; iresponsible - irresponsible; crimminal - criminal; disorderley - disorderly; deterrant - deterrent

B1* a) practice - The doctor's practice was in the main street.
b) practise - I must practise my music to improve.
c) beat - I will beat you in the cross-country race.
d) bet - I bet I will come first in the race.
e) affect - His teasing did affect her confidence.
f) effect - The effect of putting a blind in the window was to cut out the sun.

✓ Checkpoint : - *If the word you want is a verb and means change, write 'affect'. In all other places, write 'effect'.*
* examples only - student's own answers

C1 a) US - programme b) NZ
c) NZ d) US - analyse
e) NZ f) US - gaol
g) US - traveller h) NZ
i) US - aluminium

D1 a) paua b) kumara c) rangatira
d) kuia e) whero f) Ra Tapu
g) kereru h) whare i) ika

Page 40 - Punctuation

A1* a) A full stop is used at the end of a sentence and also indicates abbreviations.
b) A comma is used to separate words listed, phrases, and to indicate a pause in reading pace.
c) A semicolon shows a more pronounced pause than a comma.
d) A colon is used before a list of items.
e) A question mark indicates the sentence is a question.
f) An exclamation mark is used after a short, sharp emotional sentence.
g) An apostrophe of possession shows that someone is the owner.
h) An apostrophe of omission shows that letters have been missed out
i) Inverted commas are used to show the actual words spoken.
j) Brackets are a pair of marks used to enclose additional information in a sentence.
* examples only - student's own answers

B1 Teenagers are forever giving excuses. It appears that the moment they enter those 'teen' years a whole set of different rules applies. These rules relate to doing homework, making beds, keeping their room tidy or eating proper meals. Every request is responded to with varying excuses that stretch the patience of parents. Teenagers, who would want them?

C1 a) "Sarah has gone to the movies," said Sarah's mother.
b) "Who has she gone with?" asked Emma.
c) "I think she was meeting Paul," replied Sarah's mother.
d) 'Do you think she would mind if I met them there?" queried Emma.
e) "No. I'm sure that would be fine."
f) "I'll catch a bus into town," said Emma.
g) "Look," Sarah's mother declared, "I'm going into town now so I can give you a lift."
h) "That's great. Thanks."

Page 41 - Grammar

A1* a) The sun shone brightly.
b) High in the tree, birds had sung/sang/have sung.
c) In the distance a dog barked/has barked.
d) The car coughed and spluttered/was coughing and spluttering.
e) I worried long and hard about the problem.
f) I was standing, without moving, holding my breath.
g) I took my car when I went to the South Island.

B1 a) unearth b) misjudge c) devalue
d) unmask e) unhand f) disarm
g) detest h) misgovern i) unlock
j) unburden

Page 41 - Grammar -cont'd

B2 a) earthly b) judgemental c) valuable
d) masked e) handsome f) armless
g) testable h) governable i) locked
j) burdensome

B3 seal, unseal, sealable — cross, uncross, crossly
forest, deforest, forested — trust, mistrust, trustful
feat, defeat, defeated

C1 a) eligible b) contemptible c) licence
d) dessert e) beat f) tour

Page 42 - Tone

A1 Positive tone : sympathetic, romantic, cheerful, animated, enthusiastic.
Negative tone : rude, angry, arrogant, demanding, dismissive.

B1 a) seriously b) spitefully c) excitedly
d) calmly e) sympathetically f) gleefully
g) tartly h) anxiously

C1 Words in the columns: joyful, hopeful, buoyant, triumphant, gloating, distant, dismal, malicious, surly, pensive, calm, thoughtful, earnest, serene, soft, abusive, haughty, tranquil.

T	R	I	U	M	P	H	A	N	T	L	O
N	L	I	U	Q	N	A	R	T	H	C	K
A	B	U	S	I	V	E	I	N	O	E	A
Y	S	U	R	L	Y	T	H	G	U	A	H
O	O	G	N	I	T	A	O	L	G	R	L
U	F	L	L	U	F	E	P	O	H	N	U
B	T	L	D	I	S	M	A	L	T	E	F
D	I	S	T	A	N	T	M	D	F	S	Y
E	V	I	S	N	E	P	L	I	U	T	O
R	S	E	R	E	N	E	A	E	L	C	J
T	I	O	S	U	O	I	C	I	L	A	M

Page 43 - Appropriate Language

A1 a) native b) best c) help
d) part e) show f) boundaries
g) use h) workable

A2 Jargon is a specialized language used among members of a trade, profession or group. Jargon is indispensable to those who use it in the context of their work.

B1 a) The neighbours had just bought a used car.
b) Because of company reorganisation Peter had lost his job.
c) During investigations the factory was found responsible for a chemical spill.
d) The army retreated.

C1* a) Cliche - a cliche is an overused phrase. e.g. 'We must all stand up and be counted.'
b) Slang - slang is informal language e.g. 'He gets wasted every weekend.'
c) Euphemism - the substitution of a mild term for an offensive one, e.g. 'passed away' instead of 'died'.
d) Idiom - a form of expression using words in an unusual way, e.g. 'Henry was over the moon to win the scholarship.'
* examples only - student's own answers

Page 44 - Redundant Words

A1 a) We must co-operate.
b) The factory was close to the river.
c) When travelling it is important to take only the essentials.
d) It is true that New Zealanders have a highly competitive spirit.
e) The audience at the play began to squirm in their seats.

B1 a) The patient in the end room is mentally ill.
b) A dedicated teacher helps each student to become better academically and emotionally.
c) His skill in carving was unique.
d) Her complexion became pink as she was teased by her friends.

Page 44 - Redundant Words - cont'd

B1 e) Boys today wear clothes that are invariably too large.
f) Wallace scribbled a note to his mother on an envelope.
g) Those on the dole are often called lazy.
h) Samuel still hasn't gone to the dentist.
i) Karen was determined that she would lose weight.

C1 a) Now b) because c) for
d) Although e) finally f) to
g) like h) about i) soon
j) Congratulations

Page 45 - AS 1.2 - Test

* student's own answer
Marking Checklist : a) arguments well explained
b) well supported with facts
c) writing style appropriate to a newspaper article.
d) material organised well
e) accurate spelling
f) accurate punctuation
g) text correctly paragraphed

Page 46 - Plot

A1* student's own answers depending on text studied
B1* student's own answers depending on text studied
✓ Checkpoint : *The event you chose as a climax should have produced a clear 'winner'. In rare cases there can be two winners or two losers but in all cases, the conflict is ended by the event.*

Page 47 - Sub-Plot

A1* student's own answers depending on text studied.
✓ Checkpoint : *The characters in the sub-plot must have the same problem (e.g. betrayal, barriers to true love, a duty to revenge) as the characters in the main plot.*

Page 48 - Theme

A1* a) 'Lord of the Rings' (novel/film)
b) 'Friends' (TV show)
c) 'Pride and Prejudice' (Novel / TV drama)
d) 'Saving Private Ryan' (film)
e) 'Pygmalion' (play)
f) 'The Outsiders' (novel/film) * examples only

B1* student's own answers depending on text studied

Page 49 - Major Characters

A1* student's own answers depending on text studied.
B1* student's own answers depending on character selected.
✓ Checkpoint : a) - *Your answer should have both a 'head' and a 'heart' component (judgement and feeling) e.g. "foolish and lovable."*
C1* student's own answers depending on character selected

Page 50 - Minor Characters

A1* student's own answers depending on character selected
B1* student's own answers depending on character selected
✓ Checkpoint : - *Have you included a quotation either from or about your character?*
C1* student's own answers depending on character selected

Page 51 - Setting

A1* student's own answers depending on text studied
B1* student's own answers depending on text studied
✓ Checkpoint : - *In the text, there will be a character who accepts or rejects the values of the world he or she is in. Have you linked this acceptance or rejection to a theme?*
C1* student's own answers depending on text studied

Page 52 - Social Background

A1 Upstairs - Gentleman: well-educated, gives orders, extravagant, controlling, well-dressed.
Downstairs - Servant: takes orders, frugal, few rights, household uniform, little education.

A2 Circled: restrained, mild, agreeable, modulated, judicious.

B1* a) Caveman: aggressive, powerful, unfriendly, coarse.
b) Nurse: considerate, caring, compassionate, vigilant.
c) Maori Warrior: brave, skilful, shrewd, hostile.
d) Spoilt Child: sulky, demanding, obnoxious, impossible.
* examples only - student's own answers

C1* student's own answers depending on text studied

Page 53 - Style

A1 a) The story is about ordinary people in New Zealand.
b) Formal language used for a meeting of some kind. Formal situation.
c) A sense of fear is created.
d) There is a sense of spitefulness conveyed with the words 'raucous laughter'.

B1* student's own answers depending on text studied
C1* student's own answers depending on text studied

Page 54 - Writing a Response

A1* student's own answers depending on text studied
B1* student's own answers depending on text studied
✓ Checkpoint : *Would someone who has not read this text understand your explanation? Describe people as well as naming them.*

Page 55 - Type

A1 a) biography b) manual c) travel
d) adventure e) diary f) autobiography
g) history

B1* a) a person's life story.
b) books on cars, hobbies, sport etc.
c) books on other places or by people who have travelled.
d) books on unusual, exciting or daring experiences.
e) a book kept by a person detailing their own daily events and experiences.
f) the author's life story.
g) books about the past. * examples only

C1* student's own answers depending on non-fiction book
✓ Checkpoint : *Did you include a 'response' sentence in your answer? The higher grades require you to make a link from the text to yourself or your world.*

Page 56 - Viewpoint

A1* student's own answers depending on text studied
B1* student's own answers depending on text studied

C1 a) I sat on a bench at the park. I was watching two children playing on a slide. Suddenly one of the children fell off the ladder of the slide. I ran to help as there were no adults around supervising the children.

C2 a)* student's own answers
b)* student's own answers

Page 57 - Features of Drama

A1 a) comedy - a play intended to arouse laughter,
b) tragedy - a serious play with an unhappy ending, especially one concerning the downfall of the protagonist.
c) comedy of manners - a play that gives a satirical portrayal of behaviour in a particular social group.
d) mystery - a play dealing with a puzzling crime.
e) social comment - a play making critical comment on aspects of society.
f) farce - a comic dramatic play that includes absurd and improbable situations.
g) melodrama - a sensational dramatic play with exaggerated characters and exciting events.

Page 57 - Features of Drama -cont'd

B1 conflict - a serious disagreement or argument between characters
action - what is taking place on stage
scenes - subdivisions of an act
acts - major subdivisions of a play
denouement - the final part of a play where matters are resolved
climax - the most intense, exciting or important point
character - part played by an actor

C1* student's own answers

Page 58 - Drama Script

A1* student's own answers

✓ Checkpoints : *Did you note that the king should be wearing his crown (so the audience knows who he is from the beginning)? Did you note that the stage should be brightly lit from the entrance side (to show that it is daytime)?*

Page 59 - Conflict

A1* student's own answers depending on play studied

B1* student's own answers depending on play studied

C1* student's own answers depending on play studied

✓ Checkpoint : *How long a time did you cover in each answer? A valid answer must be limited to a single scene.*

Page 60 - AS 1.3 - Test

* student's own answer
You are required to show in your answer that you :
a) Have read an extended written text.
b) Can show an understanding of this text.
c) Can explain how you have responded to the text.
d) Are able to use evidence from the text to support comments you make in your answers.
e) Are perceptive to events that take place in the text
f) Understand what the writer is trying to convey to the reader.

Page 61 - Short Texts

A1* student's own answers depending on text studied

B1* student's own answers depending on text studied

C1* student's own answers depending on text studied

✓ Checkpoint : - *Did your response include a comment on how some aspect of real life is portrayed in the text? This is the meaning of 'response' that is used by markers.*

Page 62 - Theme

A1* student's own answers depending on text studied

B1* student's own answers depending on text studied

✓ Checkpoint : *Did you develop your theme ideas as far as possible? An excellent answer discusses how the central situation came about and what it's long term effects will be.*

C1* student's own answers depending on text studied

Page 63 - Style

A1* student's own answers depending on texts studied

B1* student's own answers depending on texts studied

C1* student's own answers depending on texts studied

✓ Checkpoint : - *Your answer should mention at least one effect of figures of speech. They make ideas clearer, pictures more vivid, feelings more involved.*

Page 64 - Narrative

A1* student's own answers depending on text studied

B1* student's own answers depending on text studied

C1* student's own answers depending on text studied

✓ Checkpoint : - *Does your answer connect the moment to one of these key responses : enjoyment, understanding, emotional involvement?*

Page 65 - Setting

A1* student's own answers depending on text studied

B1* student's own answers depending on text studied

✓ Checkpoint : *Does your setting contribute to the events that take place or influence the behaviour of the characters, e.g. A funeral on a marae.*

C1* student's own answers depending on text studied

Page 66 - Purpose

A1* a) Title: Maui and the Sun
Purpose: To show that humans may overcome the inhuman if they are united.
b) Title: Goldilocks and the Three Bears
Purpose: To show that it is not wise to go into someone else's home when they are not there.
c) Title: The Lion and the Mouse
Purpose: One good turn deserves another.
* examples only - student's own answers

B1* student's own answers depending on texts studied.

C1* student's own answers depending on text studied.

✓ Checkpoint : *Congratulate yourself if you wrote about one of these :*
i) The title names a person or thing which we find is a symbol for an important idea e.g. 'Yellow Brick Road'.
ii) The title is a quotation from the story that sums up a person or a situation e.g. 'A Sense of Belonging'.

Page 67 - Symbolism

A1* a) A rocky road: A difficult path through life, one where there are many problems to overcome.
b) Barbed wire: Confinement or imprisonment and lack of rights and freedom.
c) A lighted candle: Hope; that there is a better future.
* examples only - student's own answers

B1* a) New Zealand(er) b) 'macho man'
c) justice d) peace
e) relief for war or disaster victims - help.
* examples only - student's own answers

B2* student's own answers

C1* student's own answers

✓ Checkpoint : *You can be sure of the correctness and importance of your chosen symbol if it is clearly linked to the main character and especially to a moment of discovery or change for this character.*

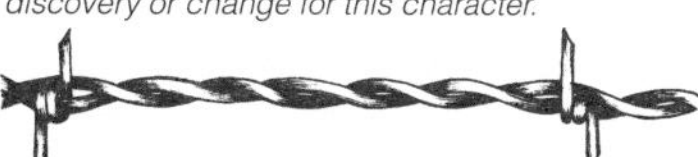

Page 68 - Climax

A1* a) climax - the most intense, exciting or important point.
b) denouement - the final part of the story in which matters are explained or resolved.
c) resolution - what happens after the climax.
d) revelation - a surprising disclosure - the revealing of something previously unknown

B1* student's own answers based on texts studied

C1* student's own answer based on texts studied

✓ Checkpoint : *If you said that one or both of your stories does not have a climax, you are correct if the main problem of the main character is still unsolved at the end of the story.*

Page 69 - Types and Stereotypes

A1* a) type - a character who does only normal things for a person in that role. e.g. mother, policeman.
b) stereotype - an image or idea of a particular type of person that has become fixed through being widely held.

A2* a) focus - particular attention
b) intensity - extreme strength or power.

B1* student's own answer

Page 69 - Types and Stereotypes - cont'd

C1* student's own answers based on text studied

✓ Checkpoint : *Your answer must explain a difference your character made to what was happening or to another person in the story. Alternatively you could have explained how the writer used the character to put across a key idea, or to create emotional responses from the reader.*

Page 70 - Responding to Text

A1* student's own answers

B1* student's own answers

C1* student's own answers

✓ Checkpoint : *Did you give a balanced answer? This means writing solidly on both parts of the question - at least 25% of your answer on each part.*

Page 71 - Language Features

A1* student's own answers

B1* student's own answers

C1* student's own answers

✓ Checkpoint : *Your answer should be about one of these : clarity, persuasiveness, vivid description, mood, emotion or entertainment.*

Page 72 - Imagery

A1 a) taste b) sight
c) smell d) hearing

B1* student's own answers based on texts studied

C1* student's own answers based on texts studied

✓ Checkpoint : *In the first part of your answer, you should have given enough detail for someone to draw the image on paper. Did you?*

Page 73 - Impact

A1* student's own answers based on text studied

B1* student's own answers based on image selected

C1* student's own answers based on image selected

✓ Checkpoint : *Effectiveness will probably come from one of these : visual contrast, idea repeated in text and image, idea contrasted in text and image, pun between text and image, meaning of text completed by image, text blended with image.*

Page 74 - AS 1.4 - Test

* student's own answer
Marking checklist :
a) clear descriptions of idea, features, images or character.
b) full explanation of importance.
c) well supported with examples and quotations.
d) personal response

Page 75 - Plot

A1* a) How the story begins.
b) The events that follow and how the characters react to those events.
c) Where the action comes to a turning point.
d) How the story ends. How it is resolved.
* examples only - student's own answers

B1* a) A sub-plot is a secondary plot that runs parallel to the main plot and may involve only some of the characters.
b) The purpose is to show another side to the characters, look at events from a different aspect or give the audience additional subtle information that may link to the main events of the text.
* examples only - student's own answers

C1* Words placed in the paragraph in this order: audience, tension, logically, believable, decisions, climax, conflict, dramatic.

D1* student's own graph based on plot of text studied

Page 76 - Major & Minor Characters

A1* student's own answers

✓ Checkpoint : *Your answer should be based on one of these two arguments : the character is convincing because he/she is like most people, or because he/she is like the particular kind of people he/she grew up with.*

B1* student's own answers

C1* student's own answers

Page 77 - Sets & Location

A1 Select 5 from these possibilities :
building styles, vehicles, clothing, hairstyles, dialogue, make-up, furniture, music, songs sung, armaments

B1* a) In the [illegible] b) Spain c) North Africa
d) Rotorua and Mokoia Island
e) On a set in a studio
* examples only - student's own answers

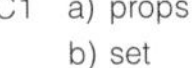

C1 a) props
b) set
c) setting
d) location
e) take
f) studio
g) exposition
h) shooting
i) credits
j) resolution

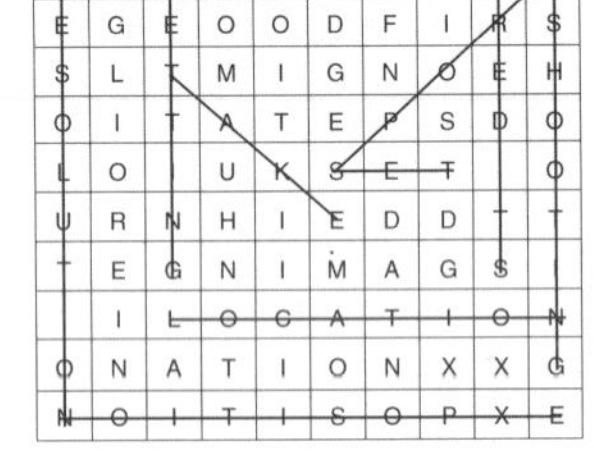

R	A	S	T	U	D	I	O	C	P
E	G	E	O	O	D	F	I	R	S
S	L	T	M	I	G	N	O	E	H
O	I	T	A	T	E	P	S	D	O
L	O	I	U	K	S	E	T		O
U	R	N	H	I	E	D	D	T	T
T	E	G	N	I	M	A	G	S	I
	I	L	O	C	A	T	I	O	N
O	N	A	T	I	O	N	X	X	G
N	O	I	T	I	S	O	P	X	E

Hidden message : A good film ignites our hidden imagination.

Page 78 - Time

A1 Real time - Same length as real action.
Story time - Shorter length than real action.
Extended Time - Longer than real action.

B1 b) A newspaper's date change.
c) Younger actor replaced by older actor
d) Stubble may grow on a man's face.
e) Shadows lengthen. f) Action speeds up.
g) Clouds / sun / moon / move faster.
h) Seasons change i) Faces age
j) Decor of a house changes - more modern
* examples only - student's own answers

C1 a) Slow Motion - The action of showing a film at a speed slower than the speed it was made at. Effect is to slow the action down. Situation e.g. - An accident is about to happen and events are slowed down to heighten tension.
b) Action Replay - A playback of part of a television broadcast, especially one in slow motion. Situation e.g. - A try is scored in a rugby match.
c) Time Lapse - A sequence of photographic frames taken at set intervals to record changes that take place slowly over time. Situation e.g. - A baby bird breaking its egg shell and struggling to emerge.
* examples only - student's own answers

Page 79 - Audience Appeal

A1* student's own answers

B1* student's own answers

✓ Checkpoint : *A common fault in answers to this question is that the 'feelings' are never named. Does your answer name pity, joy, disgust, tension or other feelings?*

C1* student's own answers

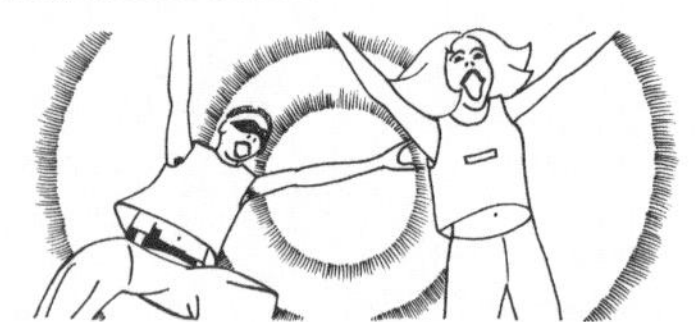

Page 80 - Camera Shots

A1*

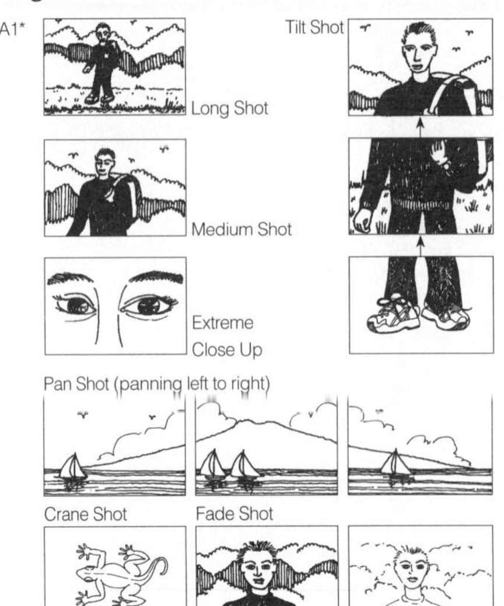

Page 81 - Camera Work

A1* student's own answers

B1* student's own answers

C1* student's own answers

✓ Checkpoint : *Did you write about tilt, pan and track shots? These are the best to cover action, but not the only ones.*

Page 82 - Filming Terms

A1 Camera Angle - High angle, low angle.
Cut-away - A shot that turns briefly from the main action.
Focus - Sharpness of an image.
Dissolve - One image fades in while another fades out.
Establishing Shot - A wide shot giving an overview of the scene so the action and setting is shown.
Deep Focus - Sharp focus from foreground to background.
Fade-in - An image gradually becomes clearer.
Flashback - A return to a scene of the past.
Freeze Frame - A single frame repeated many times.
Insert - A detail shot, Close-up of a book page, etc.
Voice-over - Narration not accompanied by an image, etc.
Out-take - A take not used in the final film.
Over-the-shoulder Shot - Often used in dialogue scenes to highlight faces.
Soft Focus - Softening the image by using filters for romantic effect.
Reaction Shot - A person's reaction to the previous action - nodding, surprise, terror.
Subjective Shot - The image may be distorted to show the character's state of mind.
Talking Heads - A scene of all talk and no action.
Tracking Shot - Camera moves on a dolly (platform) on wheels on tracks.
Two-Shot - A shot where two people are shown.
Wide Angle - Broad angle of view. Increases the sense of depth and distance.
Zoom - A shot that moves closer or retreats away smoothly from an object or person.

Page 83 - Visual Contrast

A1* student's own answers

B1* student's own answers

C1* student's own answers based on text watched

✓ Checkpoint : *A common fault of answers to contrast questions is that descriptions of two different things are given but the sentence which directly says what the difference is is absent. How did you go?*

Page 84 - Lighting

A1* student's own answers

B1* student's own answers

✓ Checkpoint : *Your answer should say that light is used to draw the eye to one person in a wide shot or that it suggests that the person in the light has special qualities.*

C1* student's own answers

Page 85 - Sound

A1* student's own answers.

B1* student's own answers. Hints from opening dialogue could include information on the setting, the season of the year, the time of day, other characters lives and the prevailing atmosphere (others).

C1* student's own answers

✓ Checkpoint : *Was the actor with the most pleasant voice and most careful diction also the most admirable character? This is part of the romantic hero/heroine stereotype.*

Page 86 - Music

A1* a) Jaws theme - Jaws
b) Titanic theme - Titanic
c), d), e) - student's own answers
* examples only - student's own answers

A2 a) Romantic - violins, flute, harp
b) Melancholy - cello, harp, pipes

B1 a) sets the mood b) builds tension
c) signals romantic moments
d) affects the emotions
e) supports the setting

C1* a) & b) student's own answers

Page 87 - Special Effects

A1* student's own answers based on film seen
A2* student's own answers based on TV programme seen.

B1* student's own answers.

✓ Checkpoint : *Special effects are usually accompanied by sound effects that reinforce the impact and strengthen the illusion by involving another sense. Is this idea in your answer?*

C1* student's own answers

Page 88 - Atmosphere and Mood

A1 a) science fiction, outer space b) romantic
c) war d) family film

A2 a) Sitar, flute b) steel guitar, ukulele
c) drums, shells

B1* student's own answers

C1* student's own answers

✓ Checkpoint : *Your answer should refer to the way the viewer becomes involved with the film e.g. feeling tension in an action film or sharing the emotions of the characters in a film about people.*

Page 89 - AS 1.5 - Test

* student's own answer
Marking checklist :
a) Shows an understanding of one visual or oral text.
b) Gives examples and quotations from the text.
c) Gives a response which relates the world of the text to the world of the student.

Page 90 - Meaning

A1* a) personal awareness
b) the way things are done in the culture of Samoa
* examples only - student's own answers

B1* a) The use of a moko design and a stylised map of New Zealand indicates a poster directed at New Zealand Maori issues. The slogan 'We are Aotearoa' shows the strength of purpose the organisation desires to present.
* example only - student's own answer

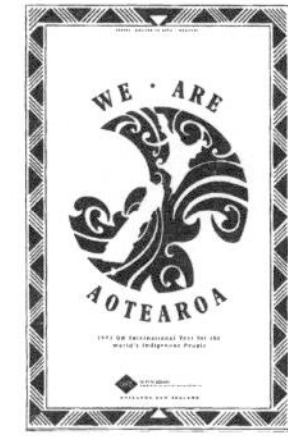

C1 a) The pig who built the brick house
b) Conversational, smug, superior
c) Words such as: stop fooling around, alright, crummy, yellow shack, contracted words : you're, don't, I'd
d) Repeating the word "brick" makes the remark authoritative and shows the narrator is sure of what he is talking about.
e) The house of straw

Page 91 - Style

A1* a) Our future is of the utmost importance and we must invest in this.
b) Please think carefully and consider how important this will be for your future.
c) Got a great scheme for your old age you can splash your dollars on.
d) Don't turn your back on this opportunity I'm giving you to look after yourself in your old age.
e) Without investing in your future now you are without any security at all
* examples only - student's own answers

B1* student's own answer.

C1 student's own montage - range of styles represented

Page 92 - Types of Sentences

A1 Laura swung onto her horse.
A2 Laura swung onto her horse and she settled into the saddle.
A3 Laura swung onto her horse when she had to enter the show ring.
A4 This is a minor sentence because it has no verb/no subject.
B1 student's own sentences
B2 A phrase is a group of words which does the work of a noun, adjective or adverb.
A clause is a simple sentence which has been combined with one or more others to make a long sentence.
C1 a) "Have you seen Julie?" / "I didn't know."
b) "I wish she'd hurry up and come." / "Perhaps I'll buy some flowers and go and see her."
c) "I think she was sick last night so maybe she's unwell."
d) "Have you seen Julie?" / "Really?"
e) "I didn't know!"
f) "last night"

Page 93 - Vocabulary

A1 a) superficial / supercilious b) optician c) adolescent d) protocol e) terminal f) infection g) corrupt h) historic i) tertiary j) ultimate
B1 a) discreet, wary b) banish, remove c) active, lively d) pardon, excuse
B2 a) abuse, blame b) polite, courteous c) threaten, intimidate d) hinder, dissuade
B3 a) disappear b) unimportant c) impractical d) misconduct e) incorrect

Page 93 - Vocabulary - cont'd

B4 a) princess b) magician c) cigarette d) meaningless e) childhood
* examples only - student's own answers

C1 a) a family of young animals especially birds
to think deeply and unhappily
b) a description of an event or experience
a bill for an expense
c) relaxed and unconcerned
employed on a temporary basis

Page 94 - Parts of Speech

A1 a) Samuel Marsden, Bay of Islands
b) mission, settlers, services
c) he d) beautiful, church, early
e) established, conducted f) in, for
g) quickly
B1 a) noun b) verb c) adverb d) pronoun e) adjective f) proper noun g) preposition
C1 a) noun b) verb c) adjective d) verb e) noun f) adjective g) adjective h) noun

Page 95 - Language

A1* a) Slang - Informal language more common in speech and normally restricted to a particular context or group. e.g.s cool, mean as
b) Colloquialism - language used in ordinary or familiar language. Generally informal. e.g.s face the music, in deep strife.
c) Jargon - words or expressions used by a particular profession or group that are difficult for others to understand. e.g.s - genetic diversity (science), a network hub (computers).
* examples only - student's own answers

B1 Circled words :
skinny, sheila, crusty, ankle-biter, fuzz, wrinklies, extravagant, worn, barged, cheap.
B2* * Student's own answers
C1 a) objective b) third person c) to inform d) adults e) newspaper

Page 96 - Adjectives

A1* * student's own answers
A2* * student's own answers
A3 a) The thin lady wore a heavy cardigan.
b) Sarah was short with long straight hair.
c) The new watch was fast.
d) The apple was small and sour.
e) Cook Strait is often rough and unpleasant.
B1 famous, comfortable, sympathetic, courteous, argumentative, spectactular, microscopic, dangerous, experiemental, asthmatic
C1 Underlined Adjectives : spilt, divided, many-layered, golden, sharp, spotted, Shy, wary, gentle, Roman

Page 97 - Verbs- Tenses

A1 Verbs for Action : munched, shattered, sprawled, pounded, applauded
Verbs for Speaking : explained, mumbled, sneered, stuttered, whimpered
B1* a) hungrily, greedily b) awkwardly, heavily
c) ravenously, quickly d) confidently, steadily
e) vigorously, softly f) strongly, hurriedly
g) silently, clumsily h) joyfully, loudly
* examples only - student's own answers

Page 97 - Verbs- Tenses - cont'd

C1 a) clutches b) gathers c) flock d) Cut e) Look, leap
D1 a) I bit / I have bitten, I am biting, I will bite
b) I have driven, I am driving / I drive, I will drive
c) I have sung / I sang, I am singing / I sing, I will sing
d) I knew / I have known, I know , I will know
e) I cried / I have cried, I am crying, I will cry

Page 98 - Adverbs

A1* student's own answers
B1 a) desperately b) wearily c) abundantly d) foolishly e) courteously f) weakly g) audibly
C1 a) Where? b) When? c) How? d) Why? e) How? f) When? g) Where?
D1* student's own answers

Page 99 - Similes

A1* a) . . .unblinking eyes.
b) . . . an eagle on a crag
c) . . . brown buttons.
d) . . . as soft as a cloud,
* examples only - student's own answers

B1* a) like a lion - His father was angry and loud just as a lion is when confronted.
b) like the hand of a giant - The valley nestled in the surrounding mountains as if held in a giant hand.
c) As quick as a wink - It took only a fraction of a second to grasp the ball and go for a try.
* examples only - student's own answers

C1* A length of velvet, as if pleading, witches' hats
* examples only - student's own answers

D1 a) a bat b) a bee c) a monkey d) a pancake e) a button f) crystal, a bell g) a doorpost h) a berry i) a mouse j) a judge k) old boots l) a lemon m) thieves n) a ghost o) brass p) nails

Page 100 - Metaphors

A1* a) The wind is cold and sharp and cuts through clothing.
b) Her lips are red and sweet and small in shape.
c) The sky is very dark and starry like material with small shiny discs sewn over it.
* examples only - student's own answers

B1* student's own answers
C1 a) a fragment of glitter
b) an opening of a tunnel
c) an arcade of dreams
d) a precious stone
e) a raindrop
f) a magical flower
g) a lost fairy
C2* student's own answers

Page 101 - Personification

A1 a) rotary hoe b) bridge c) pylons d) Waves
B1* student's own answers
C1* student's own answers
✓ Checkpoint : - *Compare your endings for a) and d). There should be a menacing tone in your words for a) and a brighter, busier feel in your words for d).*
D1* student's own answers

Page 102 - Alliteration

A1* a) Grumbling and graunching
b) Plopping and popping
c) Screeching and screaming
d) Doggedly and determinedly
e) Thundering and thumping
f) Crouching and cringing
* examples only - student's own answers

B1* student's own answers

C1* student's own answers

Page 103 - Onomatopoeia

A1* a) splash, roar b) twang, pluck
c) clank, clang d) gurgle, chuckle
e) crackle, rustle f) wail, moan
g) hiss, whistle h) crackle, spit
i) chime, ticking j) creak, screech
* examples only - student's own answers

B1* a) drone b) crackle c) crunch
d) scream e) clattered
* examples only - student's own answers

B2 clatter, pluck, hiss, wash, tinkle, lap, crack, shriek, growl, gush

C1 a) crack b) rumble c) hiss
d) croak e) yelp f) zip
g) hum h) slap i) buzz
j) howl

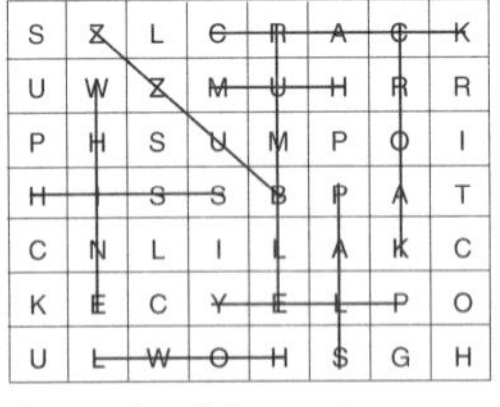

S Z L C R A C K
U W Z M U H R R
P H S U M P O I
H I S S B P A T
C N L I L A K C
K E C Y E L P O
U L W O H S G H

C2 slurp, spit, click, cough

Page 104 - Figures of Speech

A1 Simile compares one thing with another of a different kind. Uses either 'like' or 'as'.
A metaphor says one thing is another.
Personification gives human qualities to something that is not human.
* student's own examples of use

A2 Alliteration is starting two or more words with the same sound.
Assonance is the repetition of a vowel sound in nearby words.
Some things make a sound. When the word for the thing is similar this is onomatopoeia.
Rhyme is the use of corresponding sounds between words or endings of words especially in poetry.
* student's own examples of use

A3* A pun is a joke exploiting the different meanings of a word or the fact that there are words of the same sound and different meanings.
Hyperbole is a form of exaggeration not meant to be believed.
A rhetorical question is asked for effect but does not require an answer.
An imperative is an authoritative command.
* student's own examples of use

Page 105 - Hyphenation

A1 a) in-to b) with-out c) white-board
d) an-gry e) crys-tal f) crun-chy
g) frost-bite h) re-gret-ful i) lev-er-age
j) mis-tak-en

A2 a) a problem or puzzle
b) a fight or quarrel
c) a jandal, thonged sandal
d) an informal gathering
e) a successful person

Page 105 - Hyphenation - cont'd

B1 a) narrow-minded b) off-colour
c) part-time d) right-handed
e) take-off f) second-generation
g) age-old

B2* student's own answers

C1 a) mothers-in-law b) fathers-in-law
c) sisters-in-law d) brothers-in-law
e) sons-in-law f) daughters-in-law

D1 a) a person watching for forest fires
b) extremely tired
c) a delay, a violent robbery with a weapon

Page 106 - Punctuation

A1 A full stop indicates an ending.
A comma indicates the shortest pause in reading.
An apostrophe indicates possession or left-out letters.
Inverted commas are placed around spoken words or to indicate titles and extracts.
A question mark is used when a query is made.
An exclamation mark is used for a short, sharp emotional sentence.
A colon is used to introduce a series.
A semicolon is used between clauses that are closely connected to the sentence subject.
A dash is a longer mark showing a break or pause in a sentence.
A hyphen is used to join two words or for dividing a word at the end of a line.
Brackets are used within a sentence to separate an extra piece of information.
An ellipsis is a set of dots indicating the omission of words or a pause.

Page 107 - AS 1.6 - Test 1

1 I

2 To show an interruption in the sentence with a thought. To emphasise a point already made.

3 aquiline - hooked; profusely - plentifully; protruded - extended

4 A light, a candle or lamp, is being carried by someone approaching.

5 Tension is created by the sequence of events before the door is opened.
OR By using phrases such as 'heavy step approaching', 'the gleam of a coming light', 'the sound of rattling chains', 'the clanking of massive bolts drawn back' creates tension and apprehension.

Page 108 - AS 1.6 - Test 2

1 a clown

2 Condescending means showing an air of superiority.

3 The pukeko's coat is 'flashy blue' and he has 'flaunting scarlet', bright common colours in comparison to other birds.

4 The poet thinks of the common pukeko as the poor relation of the rarer, yet similar, notornis.
OR The poet describes the pukeko with words and phrases that are derogatory such as: strutting, walks in fear, ungainly, flashy, etc, while the notornis is mentioned in a restrained way which gives a dignified stature to the bird.

Page 109 - AS 1.6 - Test 3

1 Green is the best contrasting colour for red - black would also work to provide a strong visual contrast

2 The lips symbolise woman and the personal contact made between boyfriend and girlfriend.

3 The sponsors have been acknowledged by having their logo printed on the poster. Also the phrase 'in association with' is generally used to acknowledge support from sponsors.

Page 109 - AS 1.6 - Test 3 - cont'd

4 Language feature - alliteration
Phrase - 'Flappers, Fun and Frivolity'

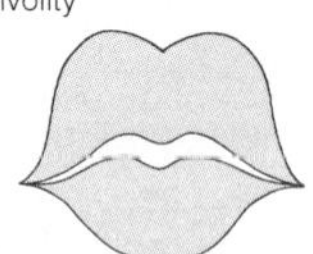

Page 110 - AS 1.6 - Test 4

1 Lines 16-17 - You can buy clothes from the children's department, pay half price at the movies and get other people to hang out the washing.

2 Pun

3 To entertain is the purpose of the speech.

4 The speaker involves the audience by asking rhetorical questions and using 'you'.

5 Repetition : To gain the attention of the audience from the beginning.
Rhetorical Question : Involves the audience. Makes them think.
Alliteration : Brings sounds into the speech and emphasises.
Proverbs : Makes the audience empathise with what the speaker is saying. Reinforces the frustration felt by the speaker.
Imagery : Brings humour in by presenting images that entertain the audience.
Contrast : Uses tall spectators to contrast with short people.

Page 111 - Topic Choice

A1* a) Cards with headings, subheadings, and notes used.
b) Made up at the time. Generally with little warning.
c) Speech prepared, learnt, then spoken from memory.
d) Reading from a text for accuracy.
e) Speech in Maori preceded by welcoming guests, thanking the hosts and greeting the living and the dead.

B1* a) Waitomo Caves - An Underground Wonderland
b) Tonga - Under Threat from Global Warming
c) Fashions in the 80's.
d) Dame Kiri Te Kanawa's Career
e) Music of the Pacific Islands
f) Protecting the Orca
g) Exploring the Amazon River
* examples only - student's own answers

C1* a) Simple language level and greetings. Keep their attention with eye-contact. Use humour. Include them with rhetorical questions.
b) Use language they are familiar with. Keep them interested. Use colloquialisms/slang sparingly.
c) Correct greetings delivered. Well-structured language - no slang. Show confidence in your knowledge of the topic. Close reiterates the purpose of the speech.
d) Respectful greetings, Polite, well chosen language. Speak clearly. Thank them for their attention.
e) Appropriate greeting. Speak in Maori or English with some Maori. Observe protocols. Appropriate close.
* examples only - student's own answers

Page 112 - Purpose

A1* student's own answers

B1* student's own answers

✓ Checkpoint : - *Are your topics suitable for a persuasive rather than a descriptive speech? "Genetic Engineering" is a descriptive topic. "Genetic Engineers are the Frankensteins of the twenty-first century" is a persuasive topic.*

B2* student's own answer

C1* student's own answers

Page 113 - Theme

A1* student's own answers

B1* student's own answers

C1* student's own answers

✓ Checkpoint : - *Answers should contain one of these :*
- Facts that are well-known or easily verifiable
- Statistics
- Logical argument
- Actual cases used as examples
- Quotation from a powerful or expert person.

Page 114 - Researching

A1* School Sources: library, teachers, other students, vertical files, archives.
Community Sources: phone book, local people, newspapers, organisations.
Library Sources: public library, National Library, librarians.
Print Sources: books, newspapers, magazines, directories, maps.
Electronic Sources: video, CDs, tapes, TV.
* examples only - student's own answers

B1* student's own answers

C1 a) statistics b) quotations c) surveys
d) interviews e) encyclopedia f) library
g) video h) newspapers i) CD-ROM
j) experts

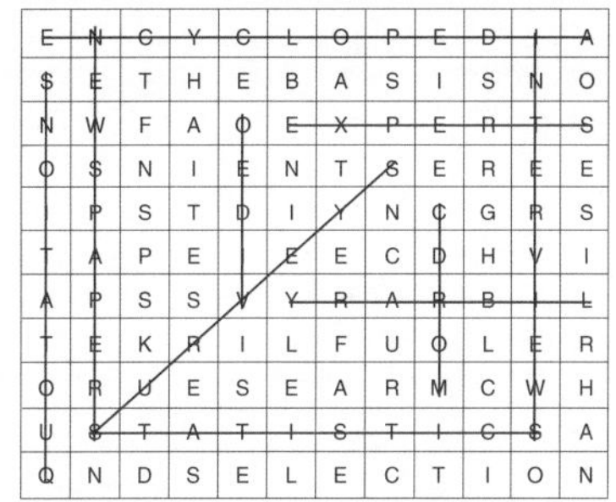

C2 Message : The basis of an interesting speech is skilful research and selection.

Page 115 - Organising

A1 a) cards b) files
c) data bases d) indexing

A2 Researching the material adds depth to the information and gives the speaker greater confidence because tthere is solid evidence to support what is said.

B1* To present a well constructed speech it is wise to arrange the material and information in order of importance with the strongest material last. Chronological order suits a speech on a subject that shows how something has developed or how an historic event has unfolded.
* example only - student's own answers

C1* student's own answers

Page 116 - The Approach

A1* a) Serious : Growing, distributing and exporting tomato products, diseases of tomatoes.
Humorous : Being a tomato and how it feels through various stages of life.
b) Serious : Evaluating the pro's and con's of examinations in the school system and in the future.
Humorous : Why bother? It's not what you know, it's who you know.
* examples only - student's own answers

B1* student's own answers

C1* student's own answers

Page 117 - Introduction

A1* a) a school assembly b) a political meeting
c) on a marae/school
d) at a debate/speech contest

A2 The audience should be informed of what the speech is about.

B1 a) audience b) topic c) attention
d) viewpoint, introductory e) points
f) entertaining

C1* student's own answers - depending on audience

Page 118 - Body

A1 a) argument b) points c) repeat
d) climax e) edit f) ideas
g) time

B1 a) Make brief notes on all ideas.
b) Group ideas into separate sections.
c) Strong ideas are best.
d) Edit ideas judiciously.
e) Make points clearly.
f) Get rid of ideas that don't fit.
g) Say those ideas in the best possible way.

C1* student's own answers based on own speech

Page 119 - Conclusion

A1 climax, summarises, lead, expressed, audience, effective, persuaded, introduction

B1* student's own answer

C1* student's own answer

Page 120 - Language Features

A1* a) Are you filled with pride that you are a New Zealander?
b) Proud? Of course I'm proud to be a New Zealander. There is much to be proud about.
c) New Zealand is a beautiful country: green of forest and field, washed by blue seas - a jewel of the South Pacific.
d) Fishing, forests, famous features and fresh air are synonymous with New Zealand's image.
e) "Be proud of who you are!"
* examples only - student's own answers

B1 a) Directly addressing audience using personal pronouns
b) Personal anecdote c) metaphor
d) colloquial language e) use of contrast

C1* student's own answer

Page 121 - Impact

A1 The ticked sentences are : a), c), e), and f).

B1* student's own answers

C1 a) . . .emotive language to make each person feel responsible for preserving their culture.
b) . . . repetition and speaking to the audience as individuals and making them feel guilty of depriving the next generation of their cultural inheritance.
c) . . . a rhetorical question to make the audience think.
d) . . . short sentences to put a personal point of view to the audience.

Page 122 - Overused Words

A1 a) pleasant, agreeable, satisfactory, good-natured, kind
b) exquisitely beautiful, very pleasant
c) imaginative, fanciful, remote and unreal
d) causing horror, likely to cause horror, very unpleasant
e) very bad, unpleasant

B1* a) elegant, graceful, attractive, fashionable, accomplished
b) tedious, dull, tiresome, uninteresting, dreary
c) enthusiastic, stimulated, passionate, animated, agitated
d) terrified, alarmed, dismayed, intimidated, horrified
* examples only - student's own answers

C1* student's own answer

Page 123 - Critical Comment

A1* student's own answers based on own speech

B1* student's own answers based on own speech

✓ Checkpoint : - *The audience can't see paragraph breaks so you have to show in the words that you have finished one point and are moving on to another. Is this clear in your draft?*

C1* student's own answers based on own speech

Page 124 - Annotating

A1 a) a typical example or appropriate model of a text
b) a selected passage from a text
c) a preliminary version of a piece of writing

B1* student's own answer

C1* a) rhetorical question
b) addressing the audience directly
c) emotive language d) use of personal pronouns
e) word choice and language level
f) sound devices, alliteration
g) figurative language h) humour
i) anecdotes j) analogies
* examples only - student's own answers

Page 125 - Delivery

A1 a) intonation b) speed c) clarity
d) volume e) emphasis

A2* student's own answers

B1 a) Stance - stand tall and comfortable. This will make you look confident and in control.
b) Notes - have all your notes in order so that you do not fumble with them.
c) Where to look - do not look at the audience in front look over their heads to the back of the room.
d) Breathing - take a few deep breaths before standing up to settle your nerves.
e) Practice - good speeches are learnt - take the time to do this - use your family for your first audience.

C1 loudness - volume, one type of speech - humorous, inflection - tone, rate - pace, a short stop - pause, stress on a word - emphasis, animated - lively, same as solemn - serious

Page 126 - Body Language

A1 a) the manner in which a person stands
b) a look on the face which indicates mood or emotion
c) movement of the hands to emphasize an idea or emotion

A2 eye, audience, gestures, stance, facial

B1 a) When the speaker disagrees with what is being said. The speaker feels the audience should not accept a particular situation either.
b) When emphasizing what is being said and the concern the speaker feels.
c) When the speaker knows the audience will agree with what is being said
d) When marking off points being presented as a list.

C1 a) blank b) confidence c) nod
d) eyes e) clench f) stare
g) point h) agreement i) gesture
j) shake k) anger l) stance

Page 127 - Presentation

A1* a) ti rakau (short sticks), music, costume
b) to e) student's own answers

B1* student's own answers based on own speech

C1* student's own answers

✓ Checkpoint : - *Did you indicate the beginning and end points of your use of the prop? Props offer the opportunity for surprise but also the danger of distraction; timing is vital.*

Page 128 - Whaikorero

A1 a) "Hello", "Thanks, may you be welcome."
b) "Welcome." "Come here."
c) "Hello" - to one person
d) "Hello" - to two people
e) "Hello" - to several people

A2 a) Pukana - stare wildly, grimace
b) Whatero - stick out tongue

B1 marae, karanga, tangata whenua, mihimihi, whaikorero, tokotoko, waiata

C1 student's own answers

Page 129 - Speech Terms

A1 a) The main purpose of a speech is to influence the audience.
b) This may be humorous, thought provoking or a greeting.
c) The speaker's angle on the topic.
d) The make-up of the audience influences the choice and level of language.

B1 a) Everyone should be able to hear including those at the back of the room.
b) Clear speech and correct pronunciation help communication.
c) Showing a range of feelings involves the audience.
d) Too fast hampers understanding, too slow is boring.

B1 marae, karanga, tangata whenua, mihimihi, whaikorero, tokotoko, waiata

C1 a) gesture b) eye contact
c) pukana d) facial expression
e) pause f) stance
g) emphasis h) whatero

Page 130 - AS 1.7 - Test

* student's own answer
Critical comments made by the students should cover each of the points listed in the test introduction:

structure — content
language features — sutiability of greeting
information provided — conclusion

Comments should be similar to those in the exemplars used by students.

Page 131 - Colour

A1 a) Red - passion, cosiness, danger, rage, excitement, heat
b) Yellow - sunlight, cheerfulness, warmth, vitality
c) Green - nature, health, calmness, peace, freshness
d) Blue - iciness, boys, water, sadness, loneliness
e) Pink - girls, femininity, calmness, gentleness
f) White - cleanliness, crispness, brides, purity, peace
g) Black - mystery, power, menace, evil, sexiness, death

B1 a) The symbol in black makes Amnesty International look like a bad thing in a good world.
b) A white symbol on a black background gives the opposite impression: a light in a dark world.

C!* student's own answers based on selected image

Page 132 - Shape and Lines

A1* student's own answers

B1* student's own answers

✓ Checkpoint : - *Did you include the use of a line of print to draw the eye to an image? This is common in ads and magazine layout.*

C1* student's own answers

Page 133 - Symbolism

A1* student's own answers

✓ Checkpoint : - *Have you made sure the symbols chosen relate only to your culture and do not cross over into another?*

B1* student's own answers

C1* student's own answers

Page 134 - Texture

A1* student's own answers

B1 a) paper b) sandpaper c) cardboard
d) crumpled paper e) foil
f) corrugated paper g) fabric
h) cellophane i) sand j) wood

C1* student's own answers

Page 135 - Lettering

A1* student's own answers

B1 Visually dominant examples are a), d), and e).

C1* student's own answers

✓ Checkpoint : - *The layout, e.g. single line or staggered lines, and the font, e.g. italic or streamlined shapes, should give an impression of speed.*

Page 136 - Layout

A1 a) The snail is no threat to the flower as it is far too small.
b) The snail, being larger, looks as if it could eat the flower.

B1

B2

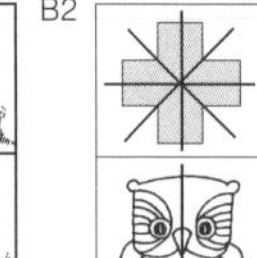

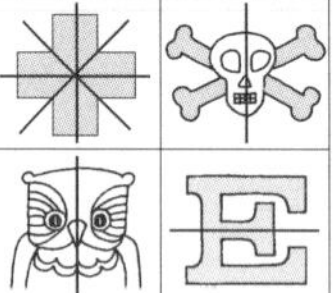

C1* student's own answers

Page 137 - Lighting

A1 a) Spotlights - focused in one area
b) Striplights - a row of coloured lights
c) Floodlights - for general illumination of the area

A2* student's own answer

B1 a) colour filters - placed over lights to give colours that affect the mood and atmosphere of the scene.
b) back light - lights the actors from behind. Gives an air of menace or power to the actors.
c) fill light - gives a soft light so shadows are not so dark. Creates a softer, more delicate atmosphere to the scene.

C1 Stage Set :
a) Shows the time and era of the play.
b) Creates an immediate overall impression to the audience.
c) Can suggest a place with minimal stage furnishings.
d) The stage set should be arranged for ease of movement.

Lighting :
a) Highlights particular actors with spotlights.
b) Creates mood and tension by the amount of light onstage.
c) Lights create various times of day or night.
d) Floods set fully with light when required.

Page 138 - Elements

A1 a) The name of the book. Generally on the second leaf.
b) Short description of a book used for promotional purposes.
c) Comments on the author's life and other work done.
d) A list of sources used by the author.

A2 a) a selected passage from the text.
b) a passage or statement repeated from a text.
c) a conversation featured in a book, play or film.
d) to do with spoken (or written) words.

B1 a) title page b) graphics c) banner
d) background e) font f) menu bar
g) links h) URL i) headline
j) images

B2 a) Visual techniques b) Verbal techniques

C1 Visual : pictures, side bar, font, costume, set, lighting, colour, shape, lettering
Verbal : voice, pause, voice-over, expression, questions, sidebar, quotations, narration, monologue

Page 138 - Elements - cont'd

C1

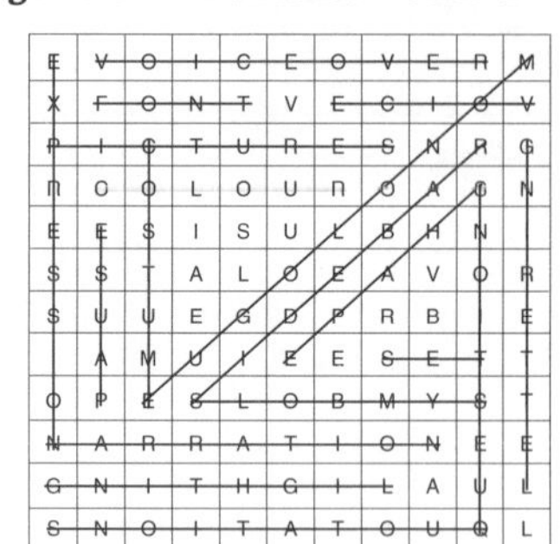

Page 139 - Language Devices

A1* a) a joke exploiting two meanings of a word
b) a deliberate exaggeration
c) statement with more than one meaning
d) a newly-coined word
e) a hackneyed or overused phrase
f) words used by a particular profession or group
g) informal words
h) expression used in ordinary conversation
i) comparing one thing with another using 'like' or 'as'
j) says one thing is another
k) same sound begins adjacent words

* student's own examples

Page 140 - Vocalisation

A1* a) Written language is generally more formal while spoken language may have contractions, incomplete sentences and colloquialisms.
b) A scripted talk has a written text which the performer either reads or has memorised fully. An impromptu speech is unplanned and unrehearsed. A scripted talk is more efficient and fluent because it has been produced with considerable thought.

* examples only - student's own answers

B1 performer, experimenting, phrases, images, natural, unlearned, conviction, attentive, purposefully

C1 Clarity - being clear, distinct,easily understood.
Projection - making your voice able to be heard from a distance.
Vitality - the state of being strong, active and energetic.
Pace - the speed with which something is said.
Confidence - faith in one's own abilities.
Naturalness - looking relaxed and real.
Pronunciation - the way in which a word is said.

Page 141 - Music

A1 a) As introduction music and again cutting in before breaks. Used at end to signal conclusion of interview.
b) Introduction music and also at the conclusion.
c) Set the scene, fade down while demonstration takes place, fills the gap while a process works and the commentary is interrupted e.g. an egg hatches, fade up at conclusion of demonstration.

B1 a) Violins, strings, harp, flutes - soft harmonious music
b) Brass bands playing military marching music
c) Music that increases in pace and rises to a climax
d) Electronic or synthesised sound
e) Mood music. Slow-paced and disquieting sounds.

C1* student's own answer

Page 142 - Sound Effects

A1* student's own answers

B1* student's own answer

Page 142 - Sound Effects - cont'd

C1 a) mystery, tension - old house
b) happiness, freedom - playing outside
c) tragedy, sorrow - storm at sea, funeral
d) nature, peace - trout fishing, bush walking
e) impatience, fury - busy city street
C2 student's own answers

Page 143 - Headlines

A1* student's own answers
B1* student's own answers
C1* student's own answers

Page 144 - Balance

A1 a) b) c) d)

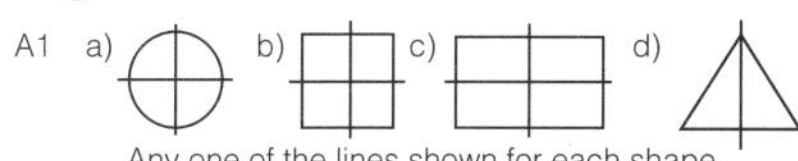

Any one of the lines shown for each shape.
A2 b) and c)
B1 b), d) and f)
C1* student's own answers
✓ Checkpoint : - *You should be able to rule a line through the centre point of the box so that one half of the layout is an approximate mirror-image of the other.*

Page 145 - Page Components

A1 a) Data corresponding to a body of writing
b) Link with other pages on the web site for more information.
c) Pictures or symbols representing programs or options that can be used .
d) A visual image on a page - supports text
e) An ad from the website's sponsor - clickable via hyperlink to sponsor's site.
f) A complete set of all the letters in the alphabet plus numerals and symbols - a style of lettering.
B1 a) specific b) innovative c) function
d) navigate e) load
C1* student's own construction

Page 146 - Character Overview

A1* student's own answers
B1* student's own answers
C1* student's own answers
✓ Checkpoint : - *Does your note on speech cover at least one of these?*
Volume (dominant or emotional character)
Diction (educated or uneducated character)
Pronunciation (Kiwi or migrant character)
Fluency (confident or unsure character)

Page 147 - Dialogue from Text

A1* student's own answers
B1* a) Introduces the character.
Briefly explains the character's general background.
Asks open questions about conflicts, crises, etc.
Brings interview to a close.
b) Gives detailed information to answer questions.
Explains situations, decisions and what was learnt.
Considers whether situations could've been handled better
Stays within role and uses expressions familiar to the character.
C1* student's own answers

Page 148 - Costume

A1* student's own answers
B1* a) gumboots, swanni, black singlet
b) a scarf, sword, eye-patch
c) dummy, bottle, bib
d) suit, pipe, magnifying glass
C1* student's own answers

Page 149 - Drama Set

A1

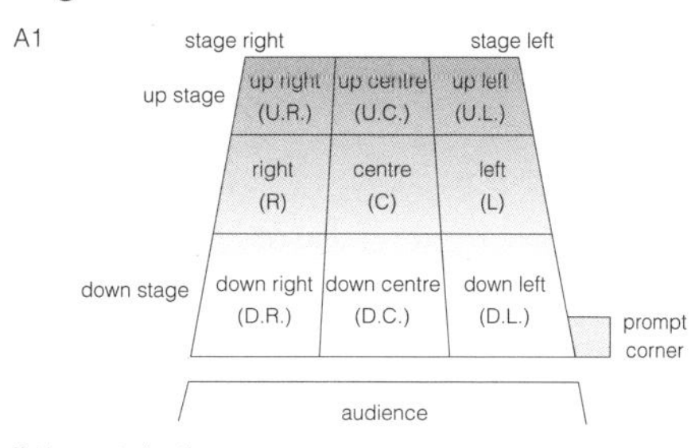

B1* student's own answers
C1* student's own answers

Pages 150/151 - AS 1.8 - Tests 1 & 2

* student's own answers
Marking checklist : a) Fully developed ideas communicated.
b) Character's feeling, personality, attitude shown.
c) Range of verbal and visual/dramatic techniques used.
d) Striking and original presentation.
e) Verbal and visual/dramatic techniques and their intended effect identified.

Page 152 - Choosing a Topic

A1* student's own answers
B1* student's own answers
C1* a), b), & c) * student's own answers
d) 2. Look at sources available to research material.
3. Make contacts / write letters early in research time.

Page 153 - Recording

A1* * student's own construction
✓ Checkpoint : - *You need to use an oral source of information. A valuable and widely-used research method is the interview, but it takes a long time to arrange, prepare for, conduct and organise for presentation. Did you allow at least two weeks?*
B1* * student's own construction

Page 154 - Brainstorming

A1* student's own answers
B1* student's own answers

Page 155 - Key Words

A1 Key words :
geography, houses, art, clothing, food, navigation
B1 Geography : volcanic islands, deep valleys, alluvial plains, coral atolls
Houses : open-sided, lashed beams, thatched roofs, circular in shape
Art : carvings, rich decorations, stone images, tattooing
Clothing : tapa, plaited fabrics, printed designs, pendants
Food : coconut, breadfruit, fish, bananas
Navigation : stars, canoes, wind, currents
C1 Key Words :
Taniwha, spirits, Hawaiiki, Maori legend.
D1* student's own answers

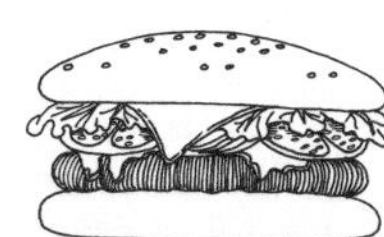

Page 156 - Key Questions

A1 a) O b) C c) C
d) O e) O f) O
g) C h) O i) C
j) C
B1* student's own answers
B2* student's own answers
C1* student's own answers
✓ Checkpoint : - *Will these questions produce balanced information to base your report on?*
For example, Question f) in Exercise A would produce valuable but unbalanced information if asked to a new immigrant, and valuable and balanced information from immigration services. Using the same question with different sources is useful to achieve balance.

Page 157 - Sources of Information

A1 Written - National Library, school archives, newspapers, reference books, pamphlets, head offices, magazines, central organisations, public library, Year Book, school library, official sources, letters, encyclopaedia, vertical files.
Visual - websites, microfiche, internet, Encarta, television, maps, posters.
Oral - teachers, extended family, local organisations, subject specialists, family members, surveys, interviews, local experts.
A2* Further sources : photographs, letters, telephone book, radio - more possible.
* examples only - student's own answers

Page 158 - Bibliography

A1 a) source - person, document etc providing information
b) format - the way something is arranged or presented
c) bibliography - a list of sources referred to.
d) author - a writer of a book, article or report.
e) publisher - a company or person who prepares books for sale.
B1* student's own answers
C1* student's own answers

Page 159 - Written Sources

A1 a) non-fiction books b) reference books c) newspapers
d) magazines e) vertical file f) CD's
g) microfiche h) archives i) search engine
j) library catalogue
B1 a) archives - old documents and records of historic importance
b) microfiche - a flat piece of film containing microphotographs of pages of a newspaper, catalogues, etc.
c) web sites - a location connected to the Internet maintains one or more web pages
d) vertical file - a file system holding newspaper and magazine articles on many topics
C1 a) fiction b) non-fiction c) Dewey
d) reference e) CD-ROM f) dictionary
g) atlas h) Year Book i) almanac
j) search engine

D	I	C	T	I	O	N	A	R	Y
A	E	K	O	O	B	R	A	E	Y
T	R	W	E	C	O	R	D	F	A
A	L	L	E	T	H	E	I	E	C
B	N	F	S	Y	O	N	R	R	D
A	M	A	A	T	I	O	O	E	R
S	N	F	L	O	U		N	N	O
E	D	I	T	N	Y	T	O	C	M
A	L	M	A	N	A	C	U	E	R
O	W	N	W	O	R		D	S	X
N	O	I	T	C	I	F	N	O	N

C2 'Record all the information in your own words.'

Page 160 - Oral Sources

A1* * student's own answers

B1 a) A survey is an investigation of the opinions or experience of people based on a series of questions.

B2 a) Include a fairly large group of people.
b) Conclusions should be drawn from survey results.
c) Choose people randomly.
d) Questions should be carefully worded.

C1 a) Pie graph b) Bar graph c) Line graph
d) Pictograph

D1 a) Write key questions.
Decide how to record the information? Writing and tape
b) Planning the questionnaire - use who, where, why, what.
Plan open questions.
c) Phone the person and explain who you are.
Explain why you want the interview and give an outline.
d) Have an interview, use a tape and take photographs.

D2 Giving their time and sharing their answers.

Page 161 - Visual Sources

A1 Select from these : photographs, cartoons, slides, art, models, maps, demonstrations, artifacts, flow diagrams, museums.

A2* student's own answers

B1* student's own answers

C1 Order : g), b), j), a), d), h), i), c), f), e).

D1* student's own answer

Page 162 - Selecting Information

A1* student's own answers

✓ Checkpoint : A1, d) - check that you have given the date for any periodical you have listed.

Page 163 - Drawing Conclusions

A1 a) A Buzzy Bee is a great child's toy.
b) These resources should be protected.
c) We must control Old Man's Beard to save the bush.

B1 a) Judgement - An evaluation e.g. that something is good or bad / important or unimportant etc.
b) Generalisation - Make a general or broad statement by inferring from specific cases.
c) Conclusion - A judgement or decision based on all the evidence.
d) Deduction - A conclusion that has been arrived at by reasoning.
e) Inference - An idea based on things that are implied rather than stated directly in the source information.

C1* student's own answers

Page 164 - Drafting

A1* student's own answer

B1 Suitable words placed into the paragraph in this order : copying, process, sources, select, drafting, findings, included.

C1* student's own answers

Page 165 - Presenting a Written Report

A1 a) Choose a topic that interests you.
b) Devise a series of key questions to research.
c) Brainstorm a range of ideas, suitable information and source.
d) Sources should cover written, visual and oral areas.
e) Collect and record information relevant to key questions.
f) Write up the report.

B1 a) Planning, collecting information, presenting.
b) Recording sources, recording information, a log.
c) The time allowance for the task; the requirements of the task; the focus of the task.

C1* student's own answers

Pages 166 - AS 1.9 - Test

* Marking checklist :
a) Report shows organisation.
b) Presented succinctly.
c) Makes generalisations.
d) Judgements are formed.
e) Report shows evidence of answering study questions.

* Assessment : 'Merit'
Has a number of generalisations.
Not enough clear, deliberate judgements for 'Excellence'.
Target questions not included.

Hints for the Exam

Before the Exam

- ❑ Review your resources for each Achievement Standard. If you have completed this book to a high standard it will be a valuable resource but you should also work from your class exercise book or folder, class handouts, marked assignments and any other marked work. In reviewing this body of work you should make summaries of the key ideas by using a highlighter, writing summaries or creating mind-maps.
- ❑ For AS 1.2, practise writing S.E.X. paragraphs on a range of issues affecting young people. These can be based on news items or media articles. Very often, the detail chosen for the X will be just what is needed to support what you say in your exam essay.
- ❑ For AS 1.3, 1.4 and 1.5, list and learn details (examples and quotations) that will support the key ideas for setting, plot, character, technique and theme.
- ❑ For AS 1.6, revise the language features used in this book and your class work. Knowledge of features relating to poetry, visual, and oral texts may be needed.

In the Exam

- ❑ Relax. You can spend half an hour on each AS and still finish early. Use your spare time to check your answers. Proofreading is especially important for AS 1.2.
- ❑ If you are nervous, begin with AS 1.6 because you can do this even during a temporary memory blank. By the time you have finished, your memory will have come back.
- ❑ Give about equal time to the Standards you are sitting. Bad time-management over two AS could result in your getting 'Excellence' for one and 'Not Achieved' for the other, when good time-management could get you two 'Achieved' grades and twice as many credits.
- ❑ Read the questions twice before you begin, and once more when you think you have finished. This helps you avoid misunderstanding the question and leaving out part of the answer.